PROPHETS, PRIESTS, AND KINGS

The Lives of Samuel and Saul

JOHN MACARTHUR

THOMAS NELSON
Since 1798

Published in Nashville, Tennessee, by Thomas Nelson. Thomas Nelson is a trademark of Thomas Nelson, Inc.

Published in association with the literary agency of Wolgemuth & Associates, Inc.

Layout, design, and writing assistance by Gregory C. Benoit Publishing, Old Mystic, CT. G_CB

Thomas Nelson, Inc. titles may be purchased in bulk for educational, business, fund-raising, or sales promotional use. For information, please e-mail *SpecialMarkets@ThomasNelson.com.*

ISBN 978-1-4185-3404-2

Printed in the United States of America

09 10 11 12 13 RRD 5 4 3 2 1

CONTENTS

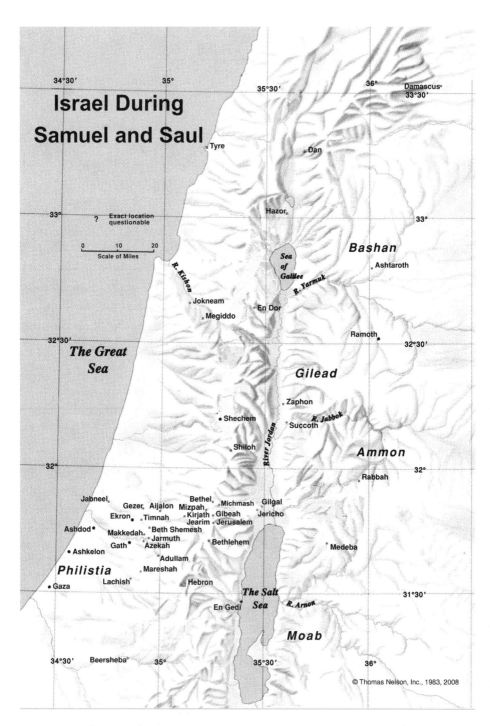

Israel During Samuel and Saul

34°30'   35°   35°30'   36°   Damascus°
33°30'

Tyre   Dan

33°   ? Exact location
questionable   Hazor°   33°

0   10   20
Scale of Miles   Sea
of
Galilee   Bashan
Ashtaroth

R. Kishon   R. Yarmuk

Jokneam   En Dor
Megiddo

32°30'   Ramoth   32°30'

The Great
Sea   Gilead

Zaphon

Shechem   R. Jabbok
Succoth

Shiloh   Ammon

32°   Rabbah   32°

Jabneel   Bethel   Michmash   Gilgal
Gezer   Aijalon   Mizpah   Jericho
Ekron   Timnah   Kirjath   Gibeah
Jearim   Jerusalem
Ashdod   Makkedah   Beth Shemesh
Jarmuth   Bethlehem   Medeba
Gath   Azekah
Ashkelon   Adullam
Philistia   Mareshah
Gaza   Lachish   Hebron
The Salt   R. Arnon   31°30'
En Gedi   Sea

Moab

34°30'   Beersheba°   35°   35°30'   36°

(FOR MORE DETAIL, SEE THE MAP ON PAGE 54.)

INTRODUCTION

The nation of Israel had been under the authority and leadership of a long series of judges for more than four hundred years, but they had grown bored with that system—even though it was the Lord's design. Looking around at the pagan nations of Canaan, Israel saw that everybody else had a king—and they wanted one of their own. Eventually, the Lord granted their demands—but He also warned the people that a king would bring with him a great deal of suffering for the nation.

In this study guide, you will meet a variety of very memorable characters. You will become acquainted with high priest Eli—and his two wicked sons. You will meet Eli's young protégé, named Samuel. You will get to know Samuel's mother, Hannah, and learn why the young boy was brought up by a priest in the temple, rather than by his family, at home. And finally, you will be introduced to Saul, Israel's first king—and his successor, David, who stood in marked contrast to his predecessor.

In these twelve studies, we will jump back and forth in chronological history, looking at one historical period and then skipping forward or backward in time as needed. We will examine Samuel's faithfulness—and Eli's *un*faithfulness. We will watch together the sad decline of Saul and the exciting rise of David. And through it all, we will learn some precious truths about the character of *God*, and we will see His great faithfulness in keeping His promises. We will learn, as did King David, what it means to walk by faith.

⌁ What We'll Be Studying ⌁

This study guide is divided into four distinct sections in which we will examine selected Bible passages:

Section 1: History. In this first section, we will focus on the historical setting of our Bible text. These five lessons will give a broad overview of the people, places, and events that are important to this study. They will also provide the background for the next two sections. This is our most purely historical segment, focusing simply on what happened and why.

Section 2: Characters. The four lessons in this section will give us an opportunity to zoom in on the characters from our Scripture passages. Some of these people were introduced in section 1, but in this part of the study guide we will take a much closer look at these personalities. Why did God see fit to include them in His Book in the first place? What made them unique? What can we learn from their lives? In this practical section, we will answer all of these questions and more, as we learn how to live wisely by emulating the wisdom of those who came before us.

Section 3: Themes. Section 3 consists of two lessons in which we will consider some of the broader themes and doctrines touched on in our selected Scripture passages. This is the guide's most abstract portion, wherein we will ponder specific doctrinal and theological questions that are important to the church today. As we ask what these truths mean to us as Christians, we will also look for practical ways to base our lives upon God's truth.

Section 4: Summary and Review. In our final section, we will look back at the principles that we have discovered in the scriptures throughout this study guide. These will be our "takeaway" principles, those which permeate the Bible passages that we have studied. As always, we will be looking for ways to make these truths a part of our everyday lives.

⤳ About the Lessons ⤲

⇻ Each study begins with an introduction that provides the background for the selected Scripture passages.

⇻ To assist you in your reading, a section of notes—a miniature Bible commentary of sorts—offers both cultural information and additional insights.

⇻ A series of questions is provided to help you dig a bit deeper into the Bible text.

⇻ Overriding principles brought to light by the Bible text will be studied in each lesson. These principles summarize a variety of doctrines and practical truths found throughout the Bible.

⇻ Finally, additional questions will help you mine the deep riches of God's Word and, most importantly, to apply those truths to your own life.

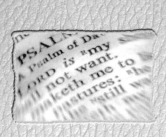

Section I:

History

In This Section:

THE FIRST PROPHET

✎ HISTORICAL BACKGROUND ✎

We open our studies at the close of the time known as the period of the judges in Israel, and the dawn of the age of the kings. The judges were individuals whom the Lord had raised up at various times and places in Israel over a period of some 350 years, beginning soon after Joshua led the people into Canaan. These judges had exercised limited authority over portions of Israel, most of them only dealing with one or two of the twelve tribes. They had frequently led Israel into battle against political enemies, and some had acted as judges in civil disputes as well—but none of them had been chosen by God to act as His prophet, speaking the words of God to the entire nation of Israel.

One reason for this might be that during those many years, there had been no one with a *whole heart* for the Lord. Perhaps He was waiting for someone who would serve Him fully and willingly. In this study, we will meet just such a person: young Samuel.

Samuel's parents had devoted him to the Lord's service prior to his birth, and from the time he was weaned he had spent his entire life living in the temple. (We will look at this further in Study 6.) He had lived as the assistant to the high priest, a man named Eli, whom he revered as a father. Yet it may surprise us to discover that, despite this upbring-ing, for much of his life Samuel did not know God in a personal way. To that end He appeared to Samuel in the dark hours one night—and Samuel answered His call with a willing heart. From that moment to the day of his death, Samuel served the Lord as His prophet in the land of Israel.

✎ READING 1 SAMUEL 3:1–21 ✎

YOUNG SAMUEL: *We meet Samuel as a youth, living in the temple, sleeping next to the ark of God, and serving the Lord full-time.*

1. THE BOY SAMUEL: Samuel was probably about twelve at this time, or possibly in his early teens. He had lived in the temple since age three and had spent his entire boy -

hood helping Eli, the high priest, minister before the Lord. Samuel's mother, Hannah, had dedicated him to the Lord's service. (We will look at her and her great sacrifice in Study 6.)

ELI: Eli was the high priest at the time, but his two sons were ungodly men. (We will consider Eli in more detail in Study 8.)

THE WORD OF THE LORD WAS RARE IN THOSE DAYS: Samuel lived at the very end of the time known as the period of the judges. He was a transitional figure, closing out the judges' period and ushering in the period of the kings in Israel. The period of the judges lasted approximately 350 years after Joshua led the people into Canaan. Prophetic revelation from the Lord was extremely limited during those years, as the Lord had chosen to reveal Himself specifically to individuals whom He called to become judges, or leaders, in Israel. The Lord was about to change His ways of revealing Himself to His people, however, making His word known more frequently in Israel through His prophet Samuel.

3. BEFORE THE LAMP OF GOD WENT OUT IN THE TABERNACLE: The golden lampstand was located in the Holy Place of the tabernacle. It was lit at twilight and kept burning until morning (Exodus 27:20–21). The Lord called Samuel to his prophetic ministry in the hours just before dawn.

GOD CALLS SAMUEL: *Samuel had served the Lord all his young life, but he still did not have a personal knowledge of God's character. That would soon change.*

4. HERE I AM: Young Samuel's response to the Lord's call gives us some early insight into his character. As he grew in his role as prophet, he learned to listen for the Lord's voice, and he was always quick to respond. Part of the reason that "the word of the LORD was rare" during the times of the judges may have been that very few individuals made themselves unreservedly available to God. The Lord may have been waiting for just such a man as Samuel, who would serve Him faithfully with a whole heart.

5. HE RAN TO ELI: There is a real poignancy in this picture of youthful Samuel running to his master, thinking that it was Eli who had called him. His quick response and humble attitude demonstrate that Samuel had a true servant's spirit, willing to leap out of bed in the darkest hours of the night to answer the call of his master.

6. THE LORD CALLED YET AGAIN: We gain some insight into the character of God as well in this passage. The Lord is not an overbearing Master, quick to punish a servant who does not respond perfectly to His call. He recognized Samuel's willing spirit and continued to call him even though Samuel misunderstood.

7. Samuel did not yet know the Lord: This statement is both an explanation and a searing indictment. It explains why Samuel was confused, for he had never heard the voice of the Lord before and therefore did not recognize it. He had served in the Lord's house his entire life, yet he did not have a personal relationship with Him at this time. And this is where the indictment lies, for it demonstrates that Eli had failed to lead his young protégé into a personal knowledge of God. Eli was the high priest, and was therefore accountable to teach Israel about God, demonstrating in his own life what it meant to walk with the Lord. But he had failed to do so.

8. Then Eli perceived: Eli's failure to teach others about God was probably a result of his own failure to walk closely with Him. He was slow to recognize God's call of Samuel because he had grown unfamiliar with His voice. This was a mistake that Samuel would *not* repeat in his own life.

Samuel's First Prophecy: *The Lord comes to Samuel and stands patiently, waiting for him to listen. Then He gives him his first word of prophecy.*

10. the Lord came and stood and called: Here we gain another profound insight into the unfathomable grace of God. Notice that He did three things here: He came; He stood; He called. The almighty God, Creator of heaven and earth, humbled Himself to come into the presence of His servant—something that no earthly king would ever do. What is more amazing is that He stood there, patiently waiting for His servant to recognize His presence—again, a reversal of earthly roles toward one's sovereign. Finally, He patiently called to Samuel, gently urging him to understand the God he served. The additional statement that He did this "as at other times" underscores the fact that the Lord is gentle and patient with all of His children, and that He humbles Himself to the role of a servant in order to bring a fuller understanding of Himself to mankind.

11. I will do something in Israel: Samuel here received his first prophecy from the Lord, and it proved to be one of his most difficult messages to deliver. Yet the Lord was giving Samuel this prophecy for the express purpose that he should tell it to others. This is always the Lord's goal when He gives His people a revelation: we are not to keep the word of the Lord to ourselves; we are to proclaim it to others.

12. all that I have spoken concerning his house: The Lord had already sent another unnamed prophet to Eli to pronounce judgment upon him and his family (1 Samuel 2:27–36). His sons were also priests at the temple, yet they were so "corrupt" that "they did not know the Lord" (1 Samuel 2:12). They were guilty of abusing their power and privileges as priests in numerous ways, including stealing from those who worshipped at the temple and committing sexual immorality. One might ask why Eli was held accountable for the sins of his children, but we must remember that he was the high priest. Those who teach God's people are held to a higher level of accountability. Eli had failed to teach the people about the God they worshipped—he had even failed to teach his own sons—and the Lord held him responsible for permitting immorality in His temple.

13. HE DID NOT RESTRAIN THEM: It is worth noting that Eli did, in fact, confront his sons about their wicked behavior (1 Samuel 2:22–25). His words were stern, but there are times when words are not enough. Eli's sons were serving at the temple of God, acting as priests and intermediaries for God's people. They were, therefore, subject to a high level of accountability, and a simple scolding was grossly insufficient in dealing with their crimes. Eli should have removed his sons from their priestly office and replaced them with men whose hearts were turned fully to the Lord. When he didn't do that, the Lord stepped in and did it for him—replacing both of the sons and Eli himself with Samuel.

14. THE INIQUITY OF ELI'S HOUSE SHALL NOT BE ATONED FOR: Numbers 15:30–31 states that "the person who does anything presumptuously . . . brings reproach on the LORD, and he shall be cut off from among his people. Because he has despised the word of the LORD, and has broken His commandment, that person shall be completely cut off; his guilt shall be upon him." The phrase translated "presumptuously" literally means "with a high hand"; that is, with disdain for the will of God. Eli had warned his sons that anyone who commits such sins cannot expect God to intercede on his behalf, for such open rebellion against God's word is a direct offense to the Lord. When Eli failed to fulfill his priestly duties by removing his wicked sons from office, he brought that curse upon his own head as well.

DELIVERING BAD NEWS: *Samuel discovers that being the Lord's spokesman can involve some heavy responsibilities—including bringing bad news to people he loves.*

15. SAMUEL WAS AFRAID TO TELL ELI THE VISION: Here is another poignant glimpse into Samuel's character. He loved his master and was loath to bring him such bad news. Yet this is part of a prophet's responsibility; he must tell others the message God has given, whether that message is good news or bad. Many Christians today shy away from telling others the truth about God's coming judgment, and some go so far as to deny that there is an eternal punishment awaiting those who reject Christ. But the gospel contains both good news (that eternal life is freely available to all who believe) and bad news (that those who reject Christ will spend eternity in hell). We do a gross disservice to unbelievers when we try to water down the Word of God.

17. GOD DO SO TO YOU: Eli recognized that a prophet risked God's anger if he did not deliver the Lord's complete message. Christians do well to keep this in mind—we are commissioned to proclaim the full gospel of Christ, not just the parts that seem pleasing to the culture around us.

19. LET NONE OF HIS WORDS FALL TO THE GROUND: This phrase contains a double meaning. On one hand, it means that Samuel's prophecies were all fulfilled by the Lord, which proved that he was a true prophet of God. On the other hand, it also means Samuel never failed to deliver God's message to His people. He recognized his high calling as the Lord's spokesman to Israel, and he treated God's word with care and respect.

20. SAMUEL HAD BEEN ESTABLISHED AS A PROPHET OF THE LORD: "When a prophet speaks in the name of the LORD, if the thing does not happen or come to pass, that is the thing which the LORD has not spoken; the prophet has spoken it presumptuously; you shall not be afraid of him" (Deuteronomy 18:22). The people of Israel knew that Samuel was speaking the word of God because his prophecies all came to pass. That same test should be applied today to those who claim to speak the word of God: if their message does not coincide with the clear teachings of Scripture, then they are not speaking a message from God.

ᗯ FIRST IMPRESSIONS ᗯ

1. *If you had been in Samuel's place, how would you have reacted to hearing your name called in the middle of the night?*

2. *Why did the Lord come to Samuel and stand before him? Why did the Lord call Samuel multiple times? What does this reveal about God's nature and His desire to save?*

3. How could Samuel have lived in the temple his entire life, yet still not know God? What does this reveal about a true saving knowledge of God?

4. Why did the Lord send such a devastating judgment upon Eli? What had he done wrong?

⌇ SOME KEY PRINCIPLES ⌇

We are called to deliver God's word faithfully— even when it seems unpleasant.

Samuel provides a glaring contrast to Eli, the high priest. Eli was responsible to ensure that the worship of the Lord was carried out according to God's commandments, yet his own sons were guilty of gross misconduct and even sexual immorality. Their sins were leading others into sin, and the Lord's name was being profaned in Israel. Yet Eli did little to stop them, and by his failure he brought God's wrath upon himself and his whole family.

Samuel, on the other hand, was always faithful to carry out the Lord's instructions, and he was willing to deliver bad news when the Lord commanded. He had spent his entire childhood in the temple, serving alongside Eli, and he loved the high priest as a father. Yet his first assignment as a young prophet was to deliver horrible tidings to Eli, a heavy responsibility for a teenager who had never before uttered a prophetic word. Nevertheless, he understood the weight of his calling and faithfully told Eli the heart-breaking news.

In a similar way, God's people are called to be a faithful testimony to the world around us, teaching others the Word of God. Our calling is similar to that of Samuel, in that we are God's witnesses in the world—and we must take care to deliver His Word accurately, even when it includes messages that are unpopular. The world does not want to hear that eternal judgment awaits those who reject Christ—for that matter, the world often gets angry when Christians teach that Jesus is the only way to salvation. But these messages are an integral part of the gospel, unpopular though they may be, and God's people need to be faithful in proclaiming the full message of what God has said.

Those who teach God's Word are called to a higher standard of accountability.

The Lord pronounced a very harsh curse upon the family of Eli, declaring that none of his descendants would live to old age. At first glance, it seems almost unfair that God would punish Eli for the sins of his sons, to say nothing of carrying that punishment into future generations. But God is never unjust, and the very severity of the sentence forces us to recognize that the Lord took Eli's failure very seriously.

Eli was complicit in the sins of his two sons because they were more important in his eyes than God Himself, and he honored them more than he honored God (1 Samuel 2:29). He did this by permitting them to carry on their vile behavior in the temple, even though it was disgracing the name of the Lord, thereby demonstrating that he cared less about God's honor than about his sons' pleasure. He had an obligation as a father to care for his sons, and he had an obligation as the high priest to care for the things of the Lord—and both those obligations required that he firmly discipline his sons for their sins.

This principle holds true specifically for those who are in spiritual leadership—James warns us, "Let not many of you become teachers, knowing that we shall receive a stricter judgment" (James 3:1)—yet it is also true in a more general sense for Christians. Those who bear the name of Christ are called to display His character to the world around us, and we are to refrain from many of the pastimes and habits in which our neighbors indulge.

The Lord is pleased by a willing heart.

Samuel was scarcely more than a boy, certainly no older than fourteen, when he heard a voice in the deep watches of the night calling his name. He leaped out of bed without complaining and rushed to his master—only to find that Eli had not called him. When he heard the voice a second time, he did not lie in bed and ignore it; he ran once again to Eli's side. When the Lord gave him some very bad news for Eli, his heart quaked at the thought of delivering such a message to the man who was like a father to him—yet he did so in obedience to the Lord, and he delivered it in full.

Eli, on the other hand, had served the Lord less willingly. When he was faced with the unpleasant task of disciplining his sons, he did not obey fully but only halfheartedly. Samuel's quick and willing obedience, even in unpleasant tasks, stood as a tacit rebuke to the high priest. We will see the same contrast later in these studies between Saul and David.

The Lord does not want His people to serve Him grudgingly, but willingly and cheerfully. "Take My yoke upon you and learn from Me," said Jesus, "for I am gentle and lowly in heart, and you will find rest for your souls. For My yoke is easy and My burden is light" (Matthew 11:29–30). And 2 Chronicles 16:9 tells us that "the eyes of the LORD run to and fro throughout the whole earth, to show Himself strong on behalf of those whose heart is loyal to Him."

ᕈ Digging Deeper ᕈ

5. Why was Samuel afraid to tell Eli what the Lord had said? What would you have done in Samuel's situation?

6. What does it mean that Samuel let none of God's words "fall to the ground"? What does this reveal of Samuel's character? Of your responsibility to God's Word?

7. Why was Eli's failure so grievous in God's eyes? What does this teach about spiritual accountability?

8. Why did the Lord have Samuel deliver a message to Eli that the priest had already heard? What did Samuel gain from this? What effect did it have on Eli?

9. Do you have a willing heart toward God? Or do you obey Him out of a sense of compulsion?

10. Have you answered the Lord's call in your own life? Have you come to a saving knowledge of Him?

2

THE LAST JUDGE

✦ HISTORICAL BACKGROUND ✦

In our previous study, we saw that Samuel was called to be a prophet in Israel. In this study, we will discover that he also served as a judge. The judges were individuals whom God called into leadership over specific segments of Israel, usually over a few of the twelve tribes. The Lord raised them up for the specific purpose of leading His people into obedience, and also to overthrow some external foe that was oppressing Israel. Many of these judges, however, were not good examples of godly behavior. Samson, for example, indulged in many forms of disobedience to the Lord's commands, including sexual depravity.

Samuel's leadership marked the end of the judges' period and the beginning of the monarchy. (We will see him anoint Israel's first king in another study.) Just as he was faithful in his role of prophet, he was also faithful in his role as Israel's last judge. He led the people to repent of their idolatrous practices, and they gained a great military triumph over their enemies under his guidance. But more importantly, Samuel demonstrated godliness in his own life, walking in obedience to the Lord's commands. The example he set in his own life was one of the most powerful aspects of his leadership as Israel's last judge.

We met the Philistines briefly in our previous study (*Finally in the Land*), but in this study we will learn more about them. They were very powerful militarily, and their armies were well trained and equipped with the most advanced weaponry. Up to now, their oppression of Israel had been relatively peaceful, but in this chapter we will see them rise up to enforce their rule with an iron hand. What is most interesting is the fact that it was while the Israelites were gathered publicly to repent of their idolatry that the Philistines were motivated to attack them.

⤙ Reading 1 Samuel 7:1–17 ⤚

Israel Laments: *The Israelites had been polluting their worship with pagan practices. Under Samuel's guidance, they turn their hearts back to God.*

1. took the ark of the Lord: The ark of the covenant was an ornate gold-covered chest with two golden angels sculpted on the top. The Lord had commanded the people to build it as part of the tabernacle during their exodus from Egypt, and it represented the presence of God among His people. The Israelites had carried the ark into battle against the Philistines when Eli was still high priest, and it had been captured and carried off to Ashdod, one of their five major cities. It had later been taken back into Israel and was being kept at Kirjath Jearim (northwest of the Salt Sea; see the map in the Introduction). See 1 Samuel 4–6 for a full account of this catastrophe.

2. it was there twenty years: That is, the ark had remained in Kirjath Jearim for two full decades by the time Samuel called the assembly at Mizpah (v. 5). The ark actually remained in Kirjath Jearim for approximately a hundred years, until David carried it back as one of the first acts of his kingship (2 Samuel 6).

all the house of Israel lamented after the Lord: During the period of the judges, the people of Israel had fallen into a cycle of sin and repentance. They would turn away from obedience to the Lord, and He would permit an enemy to oppress the nation. After a period of suffering, the people would cry out to God for help, and He would raise up a leader to serve as judge and deliverer. Under the spiritual leadership of Eli, the nation had once again turned to the pagan practices of the world around them, and the Lord had removed His hand of blessing. Under Samuel's direction, however, the nation was beginning to lament the loss of their special relationship with God.

3. put away the foreign gods: The people of Israel had added many elements of pagan religion into their worship practices, and the Lord used numerous judges to purify His people. (Gideon, for example, was called to tear down pagan idols. See Judges 6.) Israel had not utterly abandoned the law of Moses or worshiping the Lord at His temple; they had merely adulterated their worship practices with other practices from the Canaanites. The church today is in danger of this same failure, becoming fascinated with worldly entertainment and fixated with secular concepts of success, rather than sticking closely to the Word of God. But the Lord will not permit His people to create their own syncretistic religion, selecting at a whim this idea or that practice from the world's abundance of false gods. He calls His people today to "serve Him only," just as He called Israel in Samuel's time.

4. THE BAALS AND THE ASHTORETHS: Baal was a male pagan god, and Ashtoreth was female. Both were viewed by the Canaanites as holding authority over crops, fertility, and military strength. They were represented in pagan temples by statues, and Canaanite worship practices included temple prostitution and other immoral rites. The Israelites had probably incorporated both the idols and the wicked practices into their worship of God. As already noted, the Lord does not permit His people to invent their own approaches to worship, even if some worldly practices seem "culturally relevant."

SAMUEL GATHERS THE PEOPLE: *Samuel takes spiritual leadership in Israel, calling the people together for collective repentance before the Lord.*

5. MIZPAH: Located about eight miles southwest of Bethel. See the map in the Introduction.

I WILL PRAY TO THE LORD FOR YOU: Samuel demonstrated one of the important responsibilities of a prophet by interceding on behalf of others. Interestingly, there is no record of any of the previous judges offering to pray for the people.

6. DREW WATER, AND POURED IT OUT BEFORE THE LORD: Pouring out water before the Lord signified repentance (Lamentations 2:19).

SAMUEL JUDGED THE CHILDREN OF ISRAEL: Samuel is considered the last judge of Israel. He was the transitional figure in Israel's form of government, from various judges to a single king. The role of judge included leading the people in warfare and settling domestic disputes. Samuel, however, was also a prophet, and was given specific revelations from the Lord, which he communicated to the people of Israel throughout his lifetime. As we will see, his role as both high priest and prophet included acting as a counselor and advisor to the future king.

THE PHILISTINES MAKE WAR: *The Philistines feared that Samuel was organizing a revolt against them, and they gathered their armies to squash any rebellion.*

7. THE LORDS OF THE PHILISTINES WENT UP AGAINST ISRAEL: The Philistines learned that the people of Israel had gathered at Mizpah, and they feared that Samuel was leading Israel in overthrowing their rule. But the Lord's time for that overthrow had not yet come; He was more concerned that His people cleanse their lives of paganism first. God would indeed overthrow the Philistine rule, but first the people needed to repent and return to Him. The Lord ultimately used David to finally defeat the Philistines, while Samuel's role was to turn back the hearts of the people.

THEY WERE AFRAID OF THE PHILISTINES: From a human perspective, the Israelites had good reason to fear. The Philistines were a very powerful and wealthy nation, possessing five major fortified cities, each with a well-trained standing army. Their weapons were technologically advanced, while Israel's were rather primitive. Yet the people of Israel had not learned an important lesson in their relationship with God: the Lord would be faithful to fight their battles. He had defeated many overwhelming foes in the past, including the elite forces of Egypt, and He could be depended upon to do so in the future.

8. DO NOT CEASE TO CRY OUT TO THE LORD OUR GOD: Here we see that the Israelites had indeed repented of their paganism and had turned their hearts back to the Lord, referring to Him as "our God." They had also learned the important lesson that they could not use the ark of the covenant—or any other material object—as some sort of talisman to invoke the power of God at their whim. The Lord would indeed defend Israel, but He wanted His people to approach Him in prayer and obedience.

THE LORD FIGHTS THE BATTLE: *As He had done countless times in the past, the Lord sent a powerful miracle that defeated Israel's foes. Samuel sets up a monument.*

10. THUNDERED WITH A LOUD THUNDER: The Lord used a great variety of spectacular methods to beat Israel's foes. On one occasion, He caused the sun to stand still (or the earth to stop in its rotation; see Joshua 10). At other times, He rained down great hailstones or even fire from heaven. In numerous other confrontations, the Israelites did not even need to go into battle. On this occasion, He evidently sent some tremendous natural phenomenon, such as a terrific thunderstorm or perhaps an earthquake. The Philistines were stunned and confused, allowing the army of Israel to win a great victory. The Lord had shown once again that He was the one to fight for His people, and the victory was entirely His.

12. EBENEZER: Literally, "stone of help." Samuel was continuing the practice of setting up monuments to commemorate a great victory won by the Lord for His people. Joshua had the people build a pile of stones beside the Jordan River to remind them of the Lord's miracle in parting the river for them to cross on dry land. It is important to be reminded frequently of all God has done on behalf of His people, lest we forget and begin to distrust His faithfulness. This is the reason Jesus instituted the Lord's Supper, saying, "Do this in remembrance of Me" (Luke 22:19).

THUS FAR THE LORD HAS HELPED US: This does not mean, "Well, God has helped us so far—let's hope that He'll continue to do so." On the contrary, it means that the Lord had been faithful to Israel throughout the past, and the people could depend upon His continued help in the future. Samuel was teaching the Israelites that they could trust fully in the faithfulness of the Lord, and the stone memorial was a constant reminder of that fact.

13. THE PHILISTINES WERE SUBDUED: The Philistines were subdued but not utterly overcome. They did not attack Israel again during Samuel's lifetime, but they did resume their oppression during the kingship of Saul.

↳ FIRST IMPRESSIONS ↲

1. *How had the people of Israel become unfaithful to the Lord? What things needed to be purified in their lives?*

2. *Look at 1 Samuel 4:1–11. How did Israel lose the ark? Why did they take it into battle to begin with? Do you think this showed a correct or incorrect understanding of God?*

3. What circumstances and people did the Lord use to bring Israel to repentance? What was entailed in their repentance?

4. How did the Lord demonstrate His faithfulness to Israel in this passage? What was required of Israel first?

↶ Some Key Principles ↷

The Lord gives victory in the battle.

The Philistines were a very commanding nation, and their armies were feared throughout Canaan. The Israelites were armed with slings and bows at best, and many fought with simple farm tools. They were no match for the iron weapons and chariots of the mighty Philistines, and their hearts were filled with fear when the enemy gathered in force on their borders.

But their powerful foe could not stand before the wrath of God, and He sent them into confusion simply by roaring out with a thunderous voice. The Israelites still had to participate in the battle on that occasion, just as the Lord does involve His people in spiritual warfare today, but ultimately the victory belonged to Him alone.

God's people still face many foes today, whether from the open hostility of the world or from spiritual attacks of Satan—but the principle still applies: the Lord will defend and protect His people, and He can never lose. It is important to remember what He has done for you in the past, most notably in the sacrifice of His own Son on the cross at Calvary. As the apostle Paul rhetorically asked, "If God is for us, who can be against us? He who did not spare His own Son, but delivered Him up for us all, how shall He not with Him also freely give us all things?" (Romans 8:31b–32).

The spiritual battle begins at home.

The Lord did bring a tremendous victory against the Philistines, but not before His people repented of their pagan practices. The Israelites had adulterated their worship with idolatry and immorality, and they had previously been severely routed in battle against the Philistines—even to the point of losing the precious ark of the covenant. The Lord had removed His hand of blessing from His people because they were being unfaithful to Him.

The same principle applies today. The Lord is always faithful to His people, but He expects His people also to be faithful to Him. He calls us to be obedient to the teachings of Scripture and to keep our lives pure from sin. This does not mean He expects us to never fail: "For He knows our frame; He remembers that we are dust" (Psalm 103:14). It does mean, however, that we are to be quick to confess any sin, and that our lives should be growing in the image of Christ. God's concern for our practical holiness begins on the home front, as He calls us to purify our lives and walk in obedience to Him.

True leaders are examples in godliness.

Samuel stands in contrast to Eli in his leadership of Israel. Both men were appointed by God to lead His people—Eli as high priest, Samuel as a judge and prophet—but their effects on the nation were vastly different. Eli permitted his sons to act as priests under his authority, despite the fact that they were severely corrupt. He apparently did nothing to lead the nation as a whole out of idolatry and back to faithful obedience, and the ark of the covenant (the symbol of God's presence) was captured by the Philistines.

Samuel, on the other hand, did not hesitate to confront the people with their idolatry. He led the nation out of their pagan practices and back to obedience to the Lord's commands. He also interceded on behalf of the Lord's people, and God used his faithfulness to bring great blessing on Israel.

Samuel did more than just judge the people of Israel; he gave them a clear example of godliness in his own life. The only true spiritual leadership is seen in those who are examples in godliness. Praying for others, obeying the Word of God, and confessing sins are the true marks of spiritual leadership.

ᐳ DIGGING DEEPER ᐸ

5. *What worldly philosophies and practices have been embraced in Christian circles today? Which, if any, of these have you allowed into your own life?*

6. *Why didn't the Lord simply defeat the Philistines miraculously without any fighting on the part of the Israelites? What does this suggest about your own spiritual battles?*

7. In what ways does Samuel provide an example of godly leadership? Of godly obedience?

8. Why did Samuel set up the memorial of Ebenezer? What purpose did it serve for the people of Israel? For Israel's neighbors?

ᕗ Taking It Personally ᕘ

9. *Are there areas in your life that need confession and repentance? Spend time asking the Lord to show you anything that is not pleasing to Him.*

10. *What "Ebenezers" do you have to remind you of God's faithfulness? What kinds of memorials can you set up to remind you in the future?*

～ 3 ～
THE PEOPLE DEMAND A KING

↜ HISTORICAL BACKGROUND ↝

Samuel was, by now, in his sixties. He had faithfully acted as both judge and prophet in Israel for many years. He had literally devoted his entire life to serving Israel, and that service had not always been easy. At this point in his life, one might expect that he would be treated with respect and honor—but that was not the case.

Part of the problem was that Samuel's sons were repeating the same pattern as Eli's sons, abusing their power and living in wickedness. But there was also a bigger problem: the people of Israel had focused their eyes on their influential neighbors, and they were beginning to imitate men rather than God. In this chapter, the elders of Israel come to Samuel and demand that he replace himself with a king—the people wanted to be ruled by a monarchy, rather than by judges.

The Lord was not caught off guard by this demand, of course; He had plans already established for the future monarchy in Israel. But we will see that the impetus for this change of government was from the desires of the people, not from the best system established by God. The Lord knew that a kingship would bring servitude to the people; He knew they would not be happy with their choice. Sometimes it isn't good to get our heart's desires.

↜ READING I SAMUEL 8:1–22 ↝

SAMUEL'S SONS: *Samuel is now an elderly man, and his sons have families of their own. He has appointed them as judges, but they are not walking with the Lord.*

1. WHEN SAMUEL WAS OLD: Samuel was probably in his sixties at this point.

HE MADE HIS SONS JUDGES OVER ISRAEL: This was an unusual thing to do. For approximately 350 years, the Lord Himself had selected individuals to serve as His judges, and *they* did not choose their successors. We will discover, however, that Samuel's weak spot was indulging his own sons—a failing he shared with Eli, with very similar results.

2. Beersheba: Approximately forty-eight miles south of Jerusalem—see the map in the Introduction. This location had been important to Abraham and Isaac, who both dug wells there (Genesis 21; 26).

3. his sons did not walk in his ways: This is an interesting statement; one would expect to learn that Samuel's sons did not walk in the *Lord's* ways, rather than in Samuel's ways. It might possibly suggest that Samuel had failed to fully instruct his sons in the ways of the Lord, just as Eli had failed. It is important to live a life that demonstrates godliness to one's children, but that lifestyle must also be accompanied with clear instruction in God's Word. An example without instruction will lead the children to imitate the parent, but we are called to imitate Christ.

they turned aside after dishonest gain: Eli's sons were members of the priesthood, while Samuel's sons were judges, or political leaders. They did not serve at the temple, yet the effect of their corruption was all too similar to that of Eli's sons. The Lord showed grace to Samuel's family by removing the sons from power in a gentle way, rather than by the type of tragedy that Eli's family suffered.

Calling a Meeting: *The elders of Israel come to Samuel and demand he do something about the future of Israel's leadership. They want a king.*

4. the elders of Israel gathered together: The elders' request for a king was not wrong in itself. In fact, the Lord had provided instruction for this very event hundreds of years earlier: "When you come to the land which the Lord your God is giving you, and possess it and dwell in it, and say, 'I will set a king over me like all the nations that are around me,' you shall surely set a king over you whom the Lord your God chooses" (Deuteronomy 17:14–15). It is worthy of note, however, that the Lord had fully anticipated both the request for a king and the motives behind that request. Notice the wording in Deuteronomy 17:14—"I will set a king over me *like all the nations that are around me.*" The elders' request was not wrong, but their motives were.

5. you are old: This reason for demanding a king was somewhat dubious. It is reasonable, of course, to recognize that God's prophet was getting old and that his death might be imminent. (It wasn't, as it turned out.) But it is God's responsibility to raise up prophets and leaders for His people. It is not our prerogative to select those whom God anoints as shepherds of His church. Samuel may have been getting old, but the elders needed to trust that the Lord would appoint a successor in His own time.

your sons do not walk in your ways: This complaint was entirely valid. Samuel had made a mistake in this transaction, as well, by appointing his own successors, naming his sons as judges. Just as the elders were not free to select God's anointed, so also Samuel—God's anointed at the time—was not free to choose his successors.

LIKE ALL THE NATIONS: Here is the foundational reason for the elders' demand of a king: they wanted to be like the pagan nations around them. The Lord had foreseen this, as proved by the Deuteronomy passage quoted earlier, and He was not deceived by the elders' alleged motives. The people of Israel had struggled for generations to become like the world around them, and that struggle led them into idolatry and immorality again and again. Even in Saul, their first king, their desire to be like the world led to an unstable and ungodly kingship.

SAMUEL FEELS REJECTED: *Samuel is not pleased by the elders' demand for a king. The Lord is not pleased either, for they have actually rejected Him.*

6. THE THING DISPLEASED SAMUEL: Samuel was disappointed, at least in part, because he felt that he was being rejected by the people. He had literally spent his entire life serving God's people, first as a boy in the temple, later as the nation's judge and the Lord's prophet. He may also have sensed, however, the greater danger behind the request for a king: the people wanted a human leader they could see, rather than the Lord whom they could not see.

SAMUEL PRAYED TO THE LORD: Once again, we get a glimpse of the godly character of this man. When people and circumstances went against him, he did not lash out or retaliate; he turned to the Lord for help. He demonstrated the attitude that the Lord desired in all of His people: trust in Him to fight their battles and to guide them.

7. THEY HAVE REJECTED ME: God's plan for His people was that He should be their King, and that they should trust Him fully for all their needs and safety. But the people of Israel were perpetually lured away from God's plan by the ways of the world around them. The church today faces this same danger. It is easier, according to the human mindset, to trust one's future to a human being whom one can see and speak to face-to-face, but this demonstrates a lack of trust in the faithfulness and power of God.

8. ALL THE WORKS WHICH THEY HAVE DONE: The nation of Israel had repeatedly seen the power of God acting in astonishing miracles on their behalf—yet they had repeatedly refused to trust Him. What was worse, they accused the Lord of being evil, claiming again and again that He had led them out of their Egyptian slavery simply to destroy them in the wilderness or at the hands of some powerful foe. Once the Lord had settled them safely in Canaan—just as He had promised to do—they turned their hearts away from Him and embraced false gods and immoral pagan practices. The truly amazing aspect of this wretched cycle is the fact that the Lord continued to extend His grace to a nation that was so quick to reject Him as Lord.

SO THEY ARE DOING TO YOU ALSO: People who reject God's sovereignty and lordship in their lives will also reject those who serve Him. Moses was faced with the same situation, as the people of Israel repeatedly tried to remove him from leadership. Those who stand boldly for obedience to God's Word will often experience the hatred of the world.

GIVE THEM WHAT THEY DEMAND: *The Lord instructs Samuel to heed the demands of the people, giving them a king. But He also warns Israel they will not like it.*

9. HEED THEIR VOICE: This is a sobering principle: the Lord will eventually give us the things we continually clamor for—even if those things will prove harmful to us. This is not done out of a vindictive spirit; the Lord will warn us and attempt to steer us in a course that will bring blessing and godly character. But if we persist in demanding our own way, we run the terrible risk that the Lord will grant us what we demand.

10. SAMUEL TOLD ALL THE WORDS OF THE LORD: This faithfulness to God's word characterized the prophet's life. The Lord, in turn, "let none of [Samuel's] words fall to the ground" (1 Samuel 3:19).

11. HE WILL TAKE YOUR SONS: Israel had never held a standing army before the time of the kings. This set the nation apart from the world around them, particularly the Philistines, who kept a well-trained military ready for battle at all times. From a human perspective, it must have made the Israelites feel terribly vulnerable to have no organized military force prepared to meet a foe on the battlefield, but from the Lord's perspective there was no need for a standing army. It was never Israel's army that defeated her foes; it was always the Lord's mighty arm.

12. SOME TO PLOW HIS GROUND AND REAP HIS HARVEST: Israel had never experienced any centralized government before, and there had been no official "civil service." Again, this was contrary to the world around them, whose city-states included large full-time staffs that were employed by their kings. This might have sounded attractive to the Israelites at the time, but they did not realize that such employment made them vassals to their king, rather than free and self-sufficient farmers and shepherds.

HIS WEAPONS OF WAR AND EQUIPMENT FOR HIS CHARIOTS: The people of Israel commonly went into battle with short bows, slings, scythes, and other very primitive weapons. They faced enemies who boasted iron swords, heavy shields, terrifying chariots—yet they would still be victorious. Once again, the arsenal of God's people is not man-made; it is the power of God, fighting on their behalf. "For we do not wrestle against flesh and blood, but against principalities, against powers, against the rulers of the darkness of this age, against spiritual hosts of wickedness in the heavenly places" (Ephesians 6:12).

14. HE WILL TAKE THE BEST OF YOUR FIELDS: Land ownership in Israel was passed on from generation to generation as part of a family's inheritance. It was not generally bought and sold the way real estate changes hands in modern America, but was kept in the family as a sacred possession. It was a great violation of the Lord's intended system of land ownership to have a king seize one's lands for his own use.

15. A TENTH OF YOUR GRAIN AND YOUR VINTAGE: Having no centralized government also meant that the Israelites had never before paid taxes. Their entire financial obligation had been to the Lord and His temple. The "tenth" was a tithe, the percentage that a person would give to the temple or to the priests for their service. Samuel's point is that if they added a king, they would have an additional tithe to pay as well.

17. YOU WILL BE HIS SERVANTS: Samuel was warning the people that a centralized human government under a human king would actually compete with the Lord's position in their culture. The king would demand to be the people's sovereign, but only God Himself is sovereign. The king would exercise authority over every aspect of their lives—land, income, crops, livestock, even the people themselves. Central human government was not the Lord's original design for society, because the larger it grows, the more it sets itself in God's place.

18. YOU HAVE CHOSEN FOR YOURSELVES: Here again we see the principle that the Lord does permit His people to bring suffering upon themselves if they persistently demand it.

20. THAT OUR KING MAY JUDGE US AND GO OUT BEFORE US AND FIGHT OUR BATTLES: As we have seen repeatedly, these were aspects of the Lord's role in the nation of Israel. The people were indeed rejecting the Lord, demanding instead to have a mortal to lead and defend them. The more people depend upon human government, the less they depend on the Lord.

ᔛ First Impressions ᔛ

1. *Why did the Israelites want a king? Why were they unsatisfied with judges?*

2.   What part did Samuel's sons play in Israel's desire for a king? What part was played by their envy of the surrounding nations?

3.   Why was Samuel disappointed by the elders' request for a king? How would you have responded in his situation?

4.   How would a monarchy change the lives of the Israelites? What were they gaining? What were they losing?

ᴧ Some Key Principles ᴧ

It is dangerous to insist on having your own way.

Throughout their exodus from Egypt, the Israelites consistently fought against the leadership of Moses. They panicked at every obstacle and frequently accused God of having evil intentions toward them. When Moses went up the mountain to speak to God face-to-face, the people built themselves a golden idol and began to worship it. They did not want to do things God's way; they wanted to do things their own way.

The Lord raised up many judges to lead the people once they were settled in the promised land, but this was not what the people wanted. They preferred the lifestyle of their pagan neighbors, and even embraced pagan deities and immoral religious practices. Eventually, the Lord acquiesced to their demands for a king, but He did so with dire warnings of the servitude that would definitely come along with a monarchy—but still the people insisted.

God's ways may not always seem as easy or attractive as the world's ways, but they are at all times for our best interests. It is always the best course to obey the written Word of God, even if that course may seem costly at the time. In the long run, living life God's way is the best way.

Even sinful decisions fit into God's sovereign plan.

The Lord is not the author of sin, nor does He tempt His children. But God's children can sometimes be so self-willed and stubborn that He finally permits them to have their demands—even when those desires will lead to suffering. But as this passage shows, God had already made provision in the law of Moses for the day when Israel would have a king, and he even anticipated their sinful motives for doing so (Deuteronomy 17:14).

Beyond this, the kingly line God was about to establish would eventually lead to the Messiah, Jesus Himself. This is a clear example of people's sinful motives and decisions being part of God's perfect plan, which He uses to redeem those very people.

We are to follow God, not imitate the world.

The nation of Israel was surrounded by pagan nations, many of whom were very wealthy and powerful. It would have been easy to look at their Philistine neighbors and envy their prosperity and military power, and easier still to become tempted by the carnal practices seen in their pagan temples. The people may even have justified such envy with the attitude that, if the Philistines prospered by serving Baal, it can't be all that bad!

In order to imitate another person, we must be paying close attention to that person. In order to imitate the Canaanites, the Israelites had to focus their eyes on their neighbors—and that meant taking their eyes *off* of their God. What we focus on becomes our role model; if we immerse ourselves in the entertainments and lifestyles of the world, we will end up imitating the world.

Christians are to immerse themselves in the Word of God, in regular corporate worship, and in prayer. When we fill our hearts and minds with the presence and Word of God, our eyes will be steadfastly focused on Christ—and we will find ourselves imitating Him. "Therefore be imitators of God as dear children," wrote the apostle Paul. "And walk in love, as Christ also has loved us and given Himself for us, an offering and a sacrifice to God for a sweet-smelling aroma. But fornication and all uncleanness or covetousness, let it not even be named among you, as is fitting for saints; neither filthiness, nor foolish talking, nor coarse jesting, which are not fitting, but rather giving of thanks" (Ephesians 5:1–4).

Those who reject Christ will also reject His followers.

Samuel was deeply grieved when the elders of Israel demanded a king. He had devoted his entire life to serving them and serving the Lord, and he must have thought that the people were being ungrateful. He probably felt like a failure, as though his life of faithful service had been in vain.

This is a common situation for those in spiritual leadership. One may give freely and sacrificially to others, striving to obey God's Word while humbly serving in the most menial tasks—and then find that people are not satisfied. At that point, the godly servant may wonder whether his or her self-sacrifice had been in vain.

But the Lord gently reminded Samuel that those who reject Him will also reject His servants—and that principle is still true today. We are called, like Samuel, to serve the Lord faithfully and fully, while leaving the consequences in His hands. There will be times of blessing, and there will be times of suffering. But those who suffer in the Lord's service are sharing in the highest calling of all: the sufferings of Christ. "Therefore do not be ashamed of the testimony of our Lord . . . but share with me in the sufferings for the gospel according to the power of God, who has saved us and called us with a holy calling, not according to our works, but according to His own purpose and grace which was given to us in Christ Jesus before time began" (2 Timothy 1:8–9).

5. In your opinion, why did Samuel repeat the same mistake Eli had made, appointing his disobedient sons to leadership? What can we learn from their mistakes?

6. How did Samuel respond to the elders' request for a king? How does his response compare with your own response in similar situations?

7. Why did the Lord allow Israel to have a king, even though it would bring suffering? Can you think of examples of the Lord taking your own sin and sovereignly using it as part of His perfect plan?

8. Why did the Israelites want to imitate their neighbors, even after seeing the futility of serving pagan idols? What leads a person to imitate others?

⤚ Taking It Personally ⤙

9. Are you content to live as God directs, or do you tend to want things your own way? What areas in your life might the Lord want you to submit to Him?

10. Who or what do you tend to imitate in your life? What do you need to do this week to imitate Christ more closely?

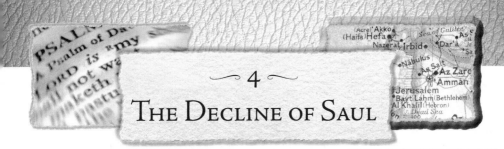

~ 4 ~
THE DECLINE OF SAUL

1 SAMUEL 13; 15

~ HISTORICAL BACKGROUND ~

The people had demanded a king, and the Lord had selected one: a young man named Saul from the tribe of Benjamin. He was tall and strong, standing head and shoulders above his peers. He was from a wealthy and influential family, and probably was among the better-educated class in his land. His family had many servants, so he was already familiar with being in a position of authority. From the world's perspective, he was well qualified to be king.

But the world's perspective is not God's perspective. Saul may have appeared kingly on the outside, but his heart was not turned toward the Lord—and that was the primary qualification for Israel's king. In fact, Saul's life demonstrated a failing that is very common in politics even today: doing what is expedient while always looking out for one's own interests.

As our passages open, Saul had been king for only two years. He had already begun to make war against the Philistines, and at first things were going well. But the day came when the battle grew fierce, and Saul's army quickly deserted. This was to be the big test of his heart: whom did Saul serve? Was he willing to submit himself to the Lord as the true King of Israel, or would he take that authority upon himself? This would be the moment when Saul would show whether or not he was a man after God's own heart.

~ READING 1 SAMUEL 13:1–15 ~

SAUL MAKES WAR: *Saul has been king for two years, and he is quick to lead the people into open war against the Philistines. In this, he is obeying the Lord's commands.*

1. SAUL REIGNED: Saul was from the tribe of Benjamin, the son of a rich and prominent man. The Lord selected him to be Israel's first king. We will look at his background and early kingship in Study 9.

2. MICHMASH . . . BETHEL . . . GIBEAH: These three locations are in the mountainous area just north of Jerusalem. See the map in the Introduction.

JONATHAN: The son of King Saul. We will look at him in Study 7.

3. GEBA: This was approximately one mile southwest of Michmash, separated by a deep ravine. The fact that the Philistines had a garrison there, near the heart of Israel, indicates the extent of their dominance over the Lord's people.

5. THIRTY THOUSAND CHARIOTS AND SIX THOUSAND HORSEMEN: This was an immense fighting force. The chariots and cavalry alone could have easily subdued Israel, whose army did not possess such powerful weapons. In fact, the small army that remained with Saul was armed mostly with farm tools—only Saul and Jonathan possessed swords, and those swords would have been of bronze rather than iron.

8. HE WAITED SEVEN DAYS: Samuel had instructed Saul a long time previously to meet him at Gilgal, where he would join him after seven days (1 Samuel 10:8).

SAUL VIOLATES GOD'S LAW: *Things in the Philistine war suddenly take a turn for the worse, and Saul finds himself in dire straits. At this point, his obedience to the Lord vanishes.*

9. HE OFFERED THE BURNT OFFERING: This was expressly forbidden by God. Only priests were permitted to offer sacrifices to the Lord, and all priests were from the tribe of Levi. It is true that Saul was in a very tight corner with his army deserting, but circumstances are never an excuse to ignore God's commands. It is a very serious matter for anyone to set aside God's requirements, but it is especially serious for those in spiritual leadership. Even today the Lord has set certain requirements on who can and cannot act in the capacity of spiritual leadership (1 Timothy 3:1–12; Titus 1:5–9). Christians should not ignore those roles any more than Saul should have violated the priestly code.

10. AS SOON AS HE HAD FINISHED: It is quite possible that Samuel waited the full seven days in order to test Saul's commitment to the Lord's commandments. Whether or not it was a deliberate test, Saul demonstrated that he was more committed to expedience than to obedience.

12. I FELT COMPELLED: Saul offered three excuses for his sin: (1) his army was scattering; (2) Samuel's appearance was delayed; (3) the Philistines were about to attack in overwhelming force. From a human standpoint, Saul merely did what he had to in a very difficult situation. But from God's point of view, difficult circumstances are never an excuse for disobedience to His Word.

14. NOW YOUR KINGDOM SHALL NOT CONTINUE: This clearly demonstrates that the Lord was testing Saul's heart in this situation. If he had remained steadfast in obeying

His commands, he would have demonstrated a heart that was committed to the Lord—and the Lord would have established Saul's lineage on the throne of Israel for all time. Instead, he proved that his heart was not committed to following God as his sovereign, and the Lord would find another man whose heart was right. That man would be David.

A MAN AFTER HIS OWN HEART: The man after God's own heart is completely committed to following the Word of God.

ᐱ READING 1 SAMUEL 15:1–35 ᐱ

GOD'S JUDGMENT ON THE AMALEKITES: *The nomadic Amalekites had attacked the Israelites on their way out of Egypt, and the Lord had sworn that He would bring judgment upon them.*

2. HE AMBUSHED HIM: The Amalekites were a wandering tribe descended from Esau, Jacob's brother. They had attacked Israel without provocation when the people were traveling from Egypt. The Lord had vowed to wipe them out as a result (Exodus 17:8–13; Deuteronomy 25:17–19).

3. UTTERLY DESTROY ALL THAT THEY HAVE: There were certain occasions when the Lord commanded His people to "utterly destroy" a city, with all its inhabitants and possessions. Such cities were "set apart" or "dedicated" to God's wrath (Deuteronomy 13:12–15). The Lord reserved certain cities for complete destruction when their hearts had become completely hardened against Him. When those cities were destroyed, the people were strictly forbidden from taking the smallest object in plunder; absolutely everything had to be destroyed—both living beings and inanimate objects—because the Lord had "set them apart" or "dedicated" them to judgment (Joshua 7).

4. NUMBERED THEM: Already the Lord's prophecy concerning kings was coming to pass, as Saul conscripted several hundred thousand men into his army.

SAUL DISOBEYS GOD'S COMMAND: *The Lord demanded that the tribe of Amalekites be wiped out completely—but Saul only obeys in part.*

9. SAUL AND THE PEOPLE SPARED AGAG: Saul committed the same sin as Achan (Joshua 7) by stealing things that were consecrated to the Lord's judgment. Achan stole only a few articles, but Saul stole on a large scale. What's worse, he led his entire army into sin.

EVERYTHING DESPISED AND WORTHLESS: This demonstrates where Saul's heart truly lay: in serving himself. It is easy to give to the Lord those things that one does not need or care about, and quite another to give Him one's best. It is also sobering to realize that the "despised and worthless" things in Saul's eyes included all the people of Amalek—except the king.

11. IT GRIEVED SAMUEL: Samuel shared the Lord's love for His people, and it grieved him that Saul had brought the Lord's anger against them. He spent the entire night crying out to the Lord on behalf of Israel and Saul. This is part of what it means to be "a man after God's own heart"—to view people and circumstances from the Lord's perspective, sharing His deep concern for others.

12. SET UP A MONUMENT FOR HIMSELF: Saul demonstrated where his true allegiance lay by building a monument to himself rather than to God. This is a stark contrast to Ebenezer, the monument that Samuel constructed to remind the people of God's great faithfulness (1 Samuel 7:12).

13. I HAVE PERFORMED THE COMMANDMENT OF THE LORD: Saul probably believed at the moment that he really had obeyed the Lord's command. After all, hadn't he killed most of the Amalekites? But partial obedience is not obedience at all; it is self-service.

15. THEY HAVE BROUGHT THEM: The moment Saul was confronted with his sin, he instantly blamed someone else—"*they* have brought them . . . the *people* spared [them] . . . [but] the rest *we* have utterly destroyed." This is a hallmark of the self-serving individual, who is quick to seek his own advantage and quick to pass the blame.

GOD REJECTS SAUL: *Saul has shown his heart is turned toward himself, rather than toward God. The Lord is about to reject Saul in favor of a man after His own heart.*

17. WHEN YOU WERE LITTLE IN YOUR OWN EYES: Saul had been very shy and hesitant to take on the role of king that was suddenly thrust upon him—to the point that he had hidden himself in a stack of military equipment on his coronation day. He had changed over time, however, as the power he wielded brought out the weaknesses in his character. This is the reason the Lord insists upon His people making Christ-likeness their first priority. David had developed godly character *before* becoming king, and that character strengthened his reign.

21. TO SACRIFICE TO THE LORD YOUR GOD: The statement in this verse is terrible in its indictment of Saul. First, he told an outright lie, saying that the people had taken the livestock specifically to sacrifice to the Lord, when in fact Saul had taken the plunder for his own gain. Even if they *had* taken the sheep for sacrifice, that still would not have excused Saul's disobedience. Saul, however, showed where his heart stood toward the Lord when he referred to Him as "the LORD *your* God" rather than "*my* God." Saul's god was his own self-will.

22. TO OBEY IS BETTER THAN SACRIFICE: Samuel dismissed Saul's claim that the sheep had been plundered for a burnt offering by cutting to the core of the issue: God wants *obedience* even more than burnt offerings or costly tithes.

23. REBELLION IS AS THE SIN OF WITCHCRAFT: Saul rebelled against God when he kept what God had told him to destroy. In so doing, what Saul really did, in effect, was reject the lordship of *his* King, submitting himself instead to the devil. Stubbornness is indeed a form of idolatry, because a stubborn person is making himself lord of his own life, insisting upon having things his own way. The modern focus on "self-esteem" is merely a contemporary form of this same idolatry.

HE ALSO HAS REJECTED YOU FROM BEING KING: God rejected Saul fairly early in his kingship, but He did not replace him immediately. Saul reigned a total of forty years.

24. BECAUSE I FEARED THE PEOPLE AND OBEYED THEIR VOICE: Even in the middle of confessing sin, Saul managed to blame other people.

26. YOU HAVE REJECTED THE WORD OF THE LORD: This is a very sobering principle that we must not miss: those who persist in rejecting the Word of God will one day be rejected *by* God. The day of grace will not last forever; *now* is the time of salvation.

29. HE IS NOT A MAN, THAT HE SHOULD RELENT: This does not mean that the Lord is not merciful; He has promised that He will remove His hand of judgment from those who repent of sin and turn back to Him. Yet, as we've already seen, the time does come when a man has no further opportunities to repent of sin. When that day arrives, the Lord's judgment on the unrepentant sinner is final and everlasting.

30. HONOR ME: In one breath, Saul both confessed that he had sinned *and* asked Samuel to honor him anyway. Once again we see that Saul's heart was fixed upon himself rather than on God, for it is God and God alone who shall receive the honor of men. (Notice also, in this verse, Saul's repetition of the phrase "the LORD *your* God.")

ᔓ FIRST IMPRESSIONS ᔐ

1.   Why did Saul make a burnt offering to the Lord? Why did Samuel react in anger?

2. If you had been in Saul's place during that fight against the Philistines, what would you have done?

3. Why did Saul not kill the king of the Amalekites? Why did he keep plunder? Why were these things sinful?

4. Why did the Lord demand the complete destruction of the Amalekites, including all their possessions? What does this reveal about the character of God?

ᒧ Some Key Principles ᒲ

God demands obedience, not expedience.

Saul obeyed the Lord's commands insofar as it suited his purposes. He attacked the Philistines in an effort to throw off their yoke of bondage, and that was in obedience to the Lord's will. But when the battle became difficult, he did not hesitate to violate the Lord's commands by usurping the authority of God's chosen priests. He attacked the Amalekites and put the people to the sword—but he kept the chosen wealth and plunder for himself.

Both of these decisions might be seen in the world's eyes as simple expedience. Saul was in an emergency with the Philistines surrounding him, and Samuel was nowhere to be found. It was simply expedient that he offer the sacrifices himself. Defeating the Amalekites was sufficient obedience; slaughtering good sheep would have been wasteful. But in both cases, Saul only obeyed in part—and he felt the freedom to choose for himself *which* part to obey.

The Lord expects His people to obey fully, not in part. Difficult circumstances do not excuse us from obedience to the Lord's commands. The Christian's job is to obey God's Word and leave the consequences in His hands. The Lord had not abandoned Saul when the Philistines surrounded him; had Saul waited for Samuel, the Lord would have worked a miraculous deliverance for Israel. He has not changed since Saul's time—He will deliver His people from destruction, yet He expects His people to obey His Word.

To obey is better than sacrifice.

Saul excused his disobedience by claiming that the people had kept the livestock in order to sacrifice them to the Lord. Even if this had been true, it would still have been disobedience to the Lord's explicit command to not take any plunder from the Amalekites.

The Lord calls His people to obey His Word, as we noted in the previous principle. This is far more valuable in His eyes than any costly sacrifice or tithe that we might bring before Him. And when we do fall into sin, He wants us to come to Him in repentance and confession, rather than with the attitude that we can somehow make up for it with good behavior. Both obedience and contrition demonstrate a heart that is turned toward God, and this is more precious in His eyes than any form of sacrifice.

Those who persist in rejecting God will one day be rejected by Him.

Saul's life was characterized by serving himself rather than God. He frequently obeyed only part of God's commands, setting his own will above God's will and effectively viewing himself as equal with God. By doing this, he was rejecting God's authority in his life.

The day came when the Lord no longer offered Saul the opportunity to repent. Saul had spoken words of repentance many times before, but his heart had never truly turned away from his sin of self-service. In time, his heart became hardened toward God, and at that point the Lord's grace became unavailable.

We are living in the age of grace, when salvation and eternal life are freely available to anyone who will repent of sin and accept God's free gift through Christ. But this day of grace will not last indefinitely; the time is coming, and may be close at hand, when Jesus Himself will return to the earth in judgment. When that day comes, those who have rejected Christ will be cast out of God's presence forever. "For He says: 'In an acceptable time I have heard you, and in the day of salvation I have helped you.' Behold, now is the accepted time; behold, now is the day of salvation" (2 Corinthians 6:2).

⤳ DIGGING DEEPER ⤶

5. *Why did the Lord reject Saul as king? What does this reveal about God's expectations for His people?*

6. In what ways did Saul make expedience more important than obedience? How did his life contrast with Samuel's?

7. If Saul had truly kept the Amalekites' livestock specifically for a sacrifice to the Lord, would that have been acceptable in God's eyes? Why or why not?

8. Look at how Samuel dealt with Agag. What lessons can be drawn from that concerning how the believer should deal with compromise and sin in his own life?

↘ Taking It Personally ↙

9. Have you accepted God's gift of salvation? If so, how do you see that in your life? If not, what are you waiting for?

10. Is your life characterized by obedience or by expedience? What area of obedience might the Lord be asking for this coming week?

ᗐ Historical Background ᗐ

The Lord had rejected Saul as king, and Saul was fully aware that He intended to anoint someone to take his place—a neighbor whose heart was devoted to God. Saul, however, did not want to relinquish the throne (a strange irony for someone who was very reluctant to accept it in the first place), and we will see later that he was willing to kill anyone who attempted to ascend to it.

Nevertheless, the Lord called upon Samuel to anoint the new king. He was to travel to Bethlehem, where he would find a man named Jesse, and the Lord would point out which of Jesse's seven sons was God's chosen. This was not the first time God had given Samuel a word of prophecy that would prove unpopular, and Samuel understandably feared for his life. In the end, however, he obeyed the Lord and headed for Bethlehem.

David was just a youth when we first meet him, yet he had already developed much godly character. He had been serving his father as a shepherd, a position involving much hard work and little honor. Yet David had not wasted that assignment, but had used his lowly position to learn many skills—including the writing of poetry and music. Those skills were about to become very useful, as the Lord called him from shepherding animals to shepherding His people.

ᗐ Reading 1 Samuel 16:1–23 ᗐ

Anointing a New King: *The Lord speaks to Samuel and urges him to stop mourning for Saul—he has a new job to perform, a new king to anoint.*

1. How long will you mourn for Saul: This visitation from the Lord probably occurred not long after Saul had been rejected as king. Samuel was mourning Saul's tragedy as one mourns for the dead, recognizing that the downfall was final and irrevocable.

I have provided Myself a king: As we saw in a previous study, the Lord chooses for Himself the ones He will anoint. The people had no say in who was to be king, and this time the Lord had chosen a young man whose heart was fully His.

2. If Saul hears it, he will kill me: Later events would show that Samuel's concerns were quite justified.

I have come to sacrifice to the Lord: The Lord was not instructing Samuel to be deceitful; He was merely adding a new focus to his trip. Samuel was to perform a sacrifice in Bethlehem instead of simply going there to anoint the new king.

4. the elders of the town trembled: The entire nation of Israel now knew that the Lord had rejected Saul and that He intended to anoint a new king. Furthermore, the people were already discovering Saul's unstable temperament (which would grow far worse), and they apparently feared a civil war.

Meeting the Sons of Jesse: *Samuel arrives at the home of Jesse and immediately thinks that the eldest son is God's chosen. But the Lord does not see as man sees.*

6. Eliab: The firstborn son of Jesse, David's eldest brother.

7. the Lord looks at the heart: It is quite likely that Eliab was a tall, handsome young man—yet Saul had also stood head and shoulders above all the men around him. Even Samuel was susceptible to the tendency of all people to judge truth based on outward appearances. We tend to believe the evidence of our senses; after all, "seeing is believing." But the fact is that seeing often leads to believing in what is *not* true, viewing things from a worldly perspective rather than from God's perspective. The Lord is not impressed with obvious accomplishments, physical appearance, wealth, or any of the things that lead to status in the world. He is only interested in whether or not a person has a heart devoted to Him.

10. Jesse made seven of his sons pass before Samuel: The firstborn son of the family traditionally had the highest honor. He would receive a double share in the inheritance, and he was viewed as the authority figure in the next generation of the family. It was only natural, therefore, that Jesse present his sons in descending order. By the time they got to the youngest, however, they were becoming perplexed.

The Ruddy Young Shepherd: *Six of Jesse's sons have been brought before Samuel, and none of them has been chosen by God. There is only one left—the youngest.*

11. keeping the sheep: The job of shepherd in David's time included a fairly nomadic lifestyle, as the flock was kept moving from one place to another in search of grazing. The shepherd would likely have been the youngest son, or even a hired hand, as it was not considered a position of prominence or honor. On the other hand, Jesse would have honored his eldest son by employing him closer to home.

12. RUDDY: That is, he had a reddish complexion, and perhaps red hair as well. The fact that David's ruddy appearance is mentioned so frequently might indicate that he was a redhead, since that was very rare among the Israelites in his day. Regardless, David was a very handsome young man—yet that was expressly *not* the reason the Lord chose him. His looks were entirely coincidental to God's selection, for God was looking solely on David's inward appearance.

13. THE SPIRIT OF THE LORD CAME UPON DAVID: Prior to the death and resurrection of Jesus Christ, God's Holy Spirit did not regularly indwell men and women. The Lord would send His Spirit upon someone such as David or the judges in order to empower them to perform some important task for the protection of Israel. There was no guarantee that the Spirit of the Lord would remain upon that person for any length of time (hence David's prayer in Psalm 51:11 that the Lord would "take not your Holy Spirit from me"); the Spirit had empowered Saul at one time, but He left him after David's coronation. Christians today, however, have the "seal of the Holy Spirit" as God's guarantee of eternal salvation, and it will never leave or depart.

GOD SENDS A TROUBLING SPIRIT: *The Spirit of the Lord has come on David, and He has left Saul. Now the Lord goes a step further and permits a demon to trouble Saul.*

14. A DISTRESSING SPIRIT FROM THE LORD: Numerous theories have been put forward concerning this phrase, including many modern perceptions of various psychological disorders. It is best, however, to take the verse at face value: that the Lord Himself permitted an evil spirit, or demon, to pester Saul. The important thing to recognize here is that the demonic force was completely subject to the will of God, yet it was not the Lord who was torturing Saul. The Lord uses the hatred of Satan and his demons to discipline His people and to punish those who are disobedient—but the Lord will never tempt anyone toward evil.

TROUBLED HIM: Saul's temperament and character were already somewhat volatile, as we have seen in our previous study. His own inconsistencies grew out of a double mind, wanting to serve both God and self. From this time onward, the Lord permitted Saul's instability to gain the upper hand, and he gradually descended into near madness. His severe bouts of depression, anger, and delusion were increased by the evil spirit the Lord had permitted to plague him.

GOD USES DAVID TO HELP SAUL: *Saul's servants quickly recognize that their king is being troubled demonically, and they suggest that he find a skilled musician.*

18. I HAVE SEEN A SON OF JESSE: There is nothing here to indicate that the person speaking was aware that David had been anointed king. From a human perspective, this suggestion was a mere coincidence. Yet there are no "coincidences" in God's eyes; the Lord deliberately brought David to mind for this job as part of His plan to place him on the throne.

SKILLFUL IN PLAYING . . . : This is an impressive list of David's character qualities. He was very skilled musically; we will learn later that he developed those skills during idle moments as a shepherd, and the book of Psalms bears testimony to his gift as a poet and songwriter. Yet he did not fit the stereotype of a poet: he was also "a mighty man of valor," having already proven his courage in combat with a bear and a lion (1 Samuel 17:36). He was a "man of war," as we will see in Study 11; and perhaps most importantly, he was "prudent of speech"—he knew when to speak and when to hold his tongue, and his conversation was edifying and encouraging. We will also see this trait in Study 11.

THE LORD IS WITH HIM: This was the very reason David had become so accomplished in so many areas at such a young age. The Lord was with David because David had already demonstrated a heart for God, an eagerness to understand and obey the will of the Lord. When a person builds his life on that attitude, the Lord will produce godly fruit.

19. SEND ME YOUR SON DAVID: Saul did not willingly give up the throne, and his later life would be spent trying to kill God's anointed king. Yet here we see that it is impossible to prevent God's will from coming to pass, as Saul invited his own successor into his inner court.

21. HE LOVED HIM GREATLY: This is a very sad passage, for it shows that David instantly loved the very king who would one day feverishly and repeatedly try to kill him.

23. THE DISTRESSING SPIRIT WOULD DEPART FROM HIM: Music can certainly have the quality of soothing troubled emotions—and it can also inflame those who are otherwise calm. But this phrase seems to indicate that the Spirit of the Lord was using David and his music to bring genuine spiritual refreshment to Saul, since the "distressing spirit" was of a demonic nature and would not have been subject to Saul's emotions. This shows us once again the mercy of the Lord, that even Saul in his unrepentant state could receive times of spiritual relief through David's service.

↠ First Impressions ↞

1. Why was Samuel afraid to travel to Bethlehem and meet Jesse's sons? How did the Lord calm his fears?

2. What qualities did David possess that prepared him to become king? How did those qualities differ from Saul's?

3. Why did God's Spirit abandon Saul? Why did He settle upon David? What does this reveal about God's priorities in your life?

4. *Why did the Lord send an evil spirit to trouble Saul? What was the Lord trying to accomplish in Saul's life?*

⌁ Some Key Principles ⌁

Man looks at the outward appearance, but the Lord looks at the heart.

When Saul was anointed king, the qualities the people noticed were that he was tall and strong, standing head and shoulders above his peers. When Samuel met the sons of Jesse, he was immediately taken by the eldest son because he, too, was tall, strong, and very handsome.

Humans tend to believe the evidence of their senses, which is unavoidable to some extent because we live in a physical, material world that is experienced through those five senses. But God transcends the things of this physical world, and He does not see our lives through five physical senses. God looks upon the hearts of people, not upon their outward appearances. He sees beyond our actions and accomplishments, weighing our hearts and looking for people who are determined to obey His Word.

It is interesting that the New Testament gives us no physical description of what Jesus looked like—how tall He was or what color His eyes were. The prophet Isaiah even tells us that "He has no form or comeliness; and when we see Him, there is no beauty that we should desire Him" (Isaiah 53:2). The Lord is not interested in such matters; He is concerned with whether we reflect the *heart* of Christ, devoting ourselves to obedience and faithfulness, and that should be the focus of all of God's people.

Even in the midst of discipline, the Lord provides help.

Saul had repeatedly rejected the word of God, refusing to obey His commands and preferring to do things his own way. As a result, the Lord had rejected him as king over

Israel, and had further subjected him to the torments of a demonic influence. Nevertheless, even in the midst of that spiritual suffering, the Lord also provided Saul with relief through his servant David.

God's discipline of Saul was intended to bring him into obedience, not to destroy him. He had lost the kingship forever, but he could still be brought back into a right relationship with the Lord—which was infinitely more important than whether or not he was king. It is also noteworthy that the Lord used David to provide the relief and encouragement, since David's heart was focused on God and was fully available to the Lord's service.

It is the same with us today. The Lord will send discipline into our lives when we persist in disobedience, but He will also provide succor. God's purpose for discipline and suffering is to draw us back to Himself when we stray, and to make us more like Christ at all times. He will use many tools and methods, including His Word and other people within the family of Christ, but His end ambition is always the same: to make us more like His Son.

Mankind cannot thwart the purposes of God.

Saul's kingship was characterized by ignoring the direct commands of the Lord, obeying the parts that coincided with his own plans while ignoring anything that did not seem expedient. He had the attitude that he was free to reinterpret the Lord's words to suit his own pleasure, and he did not recognize God's sovereignty as being greater than his own.

Yet Saul himself unwittingly furthered the very plan of God that he was trying to ignore. He would eventually spend all his efforts trying to cling to the throne that the Lord had taken away from him, but those efforts were utterly futile. He could not prevent the Lord's will from being carried out, and he ultimately even furthered those very plans against his own will.

Saul's attitude is very prevalent, even today. People often pick and choose what parts of God's Word apply to them—if any—and our culture even teaches us that we are sovereign over our own fates. We are encouraged to think that the warnings of Scripture will not apply in our own lives and that we can do as we see fit without any fear of bad consequences. But the apostle Paul wrote, "Do not be deceived, God is not mocked; for whatever a man sows, that he will also reap. For he who sows to his flesh will of the flesh reap corruption, but he who sows to the Spirit will of the Spirit reap everlasting life" (Galatians 6:7–8).

⤳ Digging Deeper ⤳

5. In what ways did Saul inadvertently advance the Lord's plan to anoint a new king? What does this reveal about God's sovereignty?

6. In what ways was Samuel guilty of looking at outward appearances in this chapter? In what ways did he step out in faith and trust God?

7. Why did God use David's music to drive away the evil spirit, when He had permitted the spirit to trouble Saul in the first place?

8. This chapter shows God sending a demonic spirit, but also sending relief from that spirit. How would you describe God's relationship to evil spirits? What did you learn about the sovereignty of God from this chapter?

⸎ TAKING IT PERSONALLY ⸎

9. When have outward appearances led you to a wrong conclusion? When have you stepped out in faith, disregarding appearances?

10. What area are you most concerned about in your own life: physical appearance or heart condition? How can you focus more on having a godly heart in the coming week?

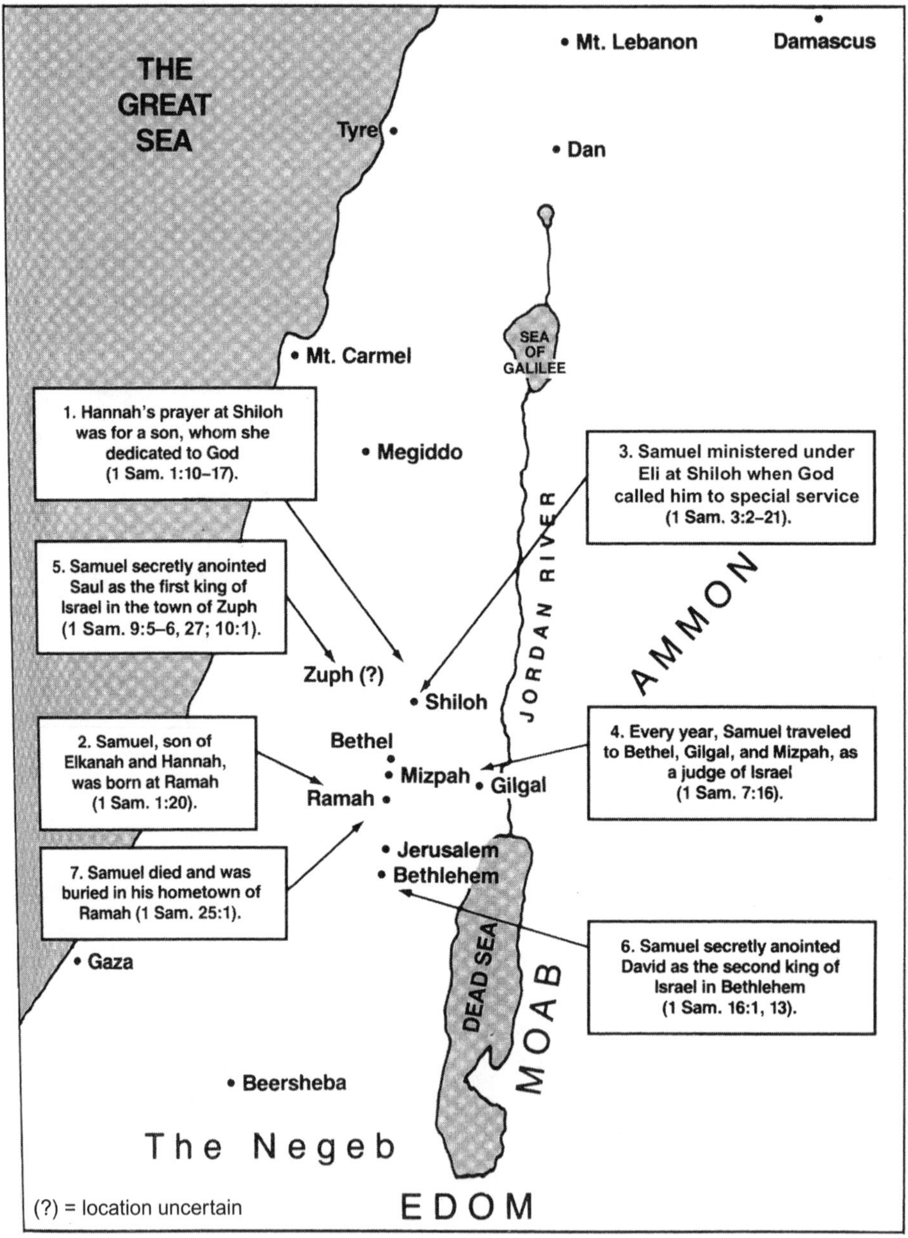
THE GREAT SEA
Mt. Lebanon
Damascus
Tyre
Dan
SEA OF GALILEE
Mt. Carmel
1. Hannah's prayer at Shiloh was for a son, whom she dedicated to God (1 Sam. 1:10–17).
Megiddo
3. Samuel ministered under Eli at Shiloh when God called him to special service (1 Sam. 3:2–21).
JORDAN RIVER
AMMON
5. Samuel secretly anointed Saul as the first king of Israel in the town of Zuph (1 Sam. 9:5–6, 27; 10:1).
Zuph (?)
Shiloh
2. Samuel, son of Elkanah and Hannah, was born at Ramah (1 Sam. 1:20).
Bethel
Mizpah
Gilgal
Ramah
4. Every year, Samuel traveled to Bethel, Gilgal, and Mizpah, as a judge of Israel (1 Sam. 7:16).
7. Samuel died and was buried in his hometown of Ramah (1 Sam. 25:1).
Jerusalem
Bethlehem
DEAD SEA
6. Samuel secretly anointed David as the second king of Israel in Bethlehem (1 Sam. 16:1, 13).
Gaza
MOAB
Beersheba
The Negeb
(?) = location uncertain
EDOM

The Life and Ministry of Samuel

SECTION 2:

CHARACTERS

In This Section:

~ 6 ~
HANNAH

↜ CHARACTER'S BACKGROUND ↝

In previous studies, we met Samuel, Israel's final judge and God's prophet to His people. He was a great man of God, and he served the Lord faithfully from his earliest childhood until the day he died. But where did such a man come from? What shaped him to become a great man of God? As the old saying goes, the apple does not fall far from the tree—who were the parents who prepared him for a lifetime of service? In this study, we will meet Samuel's parents—notably his mother, Hannah.

In Samuel's day, it was considered a disgrace for a woman to be barren. People understood that children are a gift from God, and they took that concept a step further to assume that a wife who bore no children for her husband must be under the Lord's discipline for some sin. This assumption was not true, at least not in Hannah's case, but that did not stop people from treating her with contempt when she found herself unable to bear children to her husband.

To make matters much worse, Hannah's husband had two wives—and the other wife had borne him many sons and daughters. As was quite common in such polygamous households, the two wives began to resent one another, and "the other woman" took every opportunity to ridicule Hannah for her inability to produce an heir. In general, Hannah found herself the object of great scorn and verbal abuse because of her barrenness, and her heart was filled to the breaking point with grief. But then, one day, she took her sorrows to the Lord—and that changed everything.

↜ READING 1 SAMUEL 1:1–28 ↝

AN UNHAPPY FAMILY: *Elkanah has two wives, Hannah and Peninnah. Peninnah has numerous children, but Hannah is barren. This produces strife in the home.*

1. RAMATHAIM ZOPHIM: Also called Ramah, located just south of Mizpah. (See the map in the Introduction.)

Elkanah: Meaning "God has created."

2. he had two wives: Monogamy was God's intention for mankind from the time of Creation (Genesis 2:24). Polygamy was a common practice in the ancient Middle East, but the Scriptures never endorse it.

Hannah had no children: Hannah's name means "grace," and her life became a model of God's grace. It was considered a disgrace in her day for a woman to be childless, interpreted by the world at large as a sign of God's disfavor. It only made Hannah's burden greater to be forced to live with another woman who had borne her husband numerous children. The same situation caused much grief in Jacob's household (Genesis 29–30).

3. the Lord of hosts: The word *hosts* can refer to human armies (Exodus 7:4), celestial bodies (Deuteronomy 4:19), or heavenly creatures (Joshua 5:14). The name emphasizes God's complete sovereignty over all creation, including the daily affairs of human beings, like Hannah.

5. a double portion: This was a public display of favor and honor. Joseph, for example, gave his brother Benjamin extra portions when the family congregated in Egypt (Genesis 43). Elkanah may have been intending to comfort Hannah in her barrenness, but such blatant favoritism could only produce more problems within the home.

the Lord had closed her womb: The Lord is sovereign over every event in our lives, even those things we might ascribe to natural causes. The Lord had deliberately prevented Hannah from bearing children, just as He had done with Sarah (Genesis 16:2) and Rachel (Genesis 30:2).

6. her rival: That is, Elkanah's other wife, Peninnah. It is very telling that she is not described as "Peninnah's other wife" or "Hannah's family member." Disregarding the Lord's intended family structure only brings heartache and rivalry, as we see in this case. Peninnah probably taunted and provoked Hannah because their husband was so open in his favoritism.

Hannah Turns to the Lord: *Elkanah takes his entire family to the temple at one of the annual festivals. While there, Hannah pours out her grief before the Lord.*

7. she went up to the house of the Lord: The Law demanded that all the men of Israel should appear before Him at His temple on three occasions each year. Many also took their families with them, but they were not required to do so. The fact that Elkanah also provided offerings for his wives, sons, and daughters (v. 4) indicates that he was a godly man who taught his children the ways of the Lord.

8. why do you weep: Elkanah's words were probably intended to comfort and encourage his wife, yet he could hardly have comprehended her sense of sadness and despair. His love for her undoubtedly did comfort her, yet at the same time it was also a cause of the tension between Hannah and Peninnah. In the long run, Elkanah's role as loving husband did not remove Hannah's longing for a son.

10. BITTERNESS OF SOUL: Hannah's sorrow was so great that her life felt like a bitter burden. She did not make a public display of her sorrow, however, but poured out her heart in prayer to the Lord. She was approaching the only One who could heal her heartache. Notice also that she "wept in anguish" in God's presence, rather than attempting some level of stoicism. The Lord wants His children to pour out their hearts honestly, even when they are filled with sorrow.

11. SHE MADE A VOW: It is a very serious thing to make a vow to the Lord, and should not be undertaken lightly—for God expects His people to fulfill their vows.

NO RAZOR SHALL COME UPON HIS HEAD: Hannah was referring to the vows of a Nazirite, a young man who voluntarily took upon himself specific strictures for a time of dedicated service to the Lord. The Nazirite did not cut his hair, refrained from wine, and avoided any contact with dead bodies. The Nazirite vows usually were for a limited time, several weeks or even a few months at most. Hannah was dedicating her unborn son to a lifetime Nazirite vow, dedicating him fully to the Lord's service and voluntarily giving up her rights and expectations as the boy's mother.

13. ELI THOUGHT SHE WAS DRUNK: Here is another sad insight into the character of Eli (look back a few studies for a review of his other character flaws). He was the high priest, and should have expected that people gathered in the temple were there to worship the Lord. But his own sons had corrupted the temple with their wickedness, and it may even have been fairly common for Eli to see people acting with irreverence during times of worship. He assumed the worst because his own heart was not dedicated to the Lord's service.

15. I AM A WOMAN OF SORROWFUL SPIRIT: It is tragic that Hannah was forced to defend her private prayers before the high priest himself, the one man who ought to have been her intercessor and defender.

16. OUT OF THE ABUNDANCE OF MY COMPLAINT: Hannah was doing exactly what the Lord wanted her to do, pouring out her heart's burden before Him. God wants the same from us today. And what's more, Christians have the full assistance of the Holy Spirit in pouring out our concerns to the Father. "The Spirit . . . helps in our weaknesses," Paul wrote. "For we do not know what we should pray for as we ought, but the Spirit Himself makes intercession for us with groanings which cannot be uttered" (Romans 8:26).

THE LORD ANSWERS: *Once Eli understands the situation, he blesses Hannah— and she takes that as a promise from the Lord that He will grant her plea.*

18. HER FACE WAS NO LONGER SAD: Hannah demonstrated great faith at this moment. She had poured out her heart to the Lord, and she had received an answer. She accepted Eli's word of blessing as a promise from the Lord, demonstrating her own faith in His faithful character. In this, she was like Abraham, who believed the promise of God that he would receive a son: "And he believed in the LORD, and He accounted it to him for righteousness" (Genesis 15:6).

20. SAMUEL: The name means "name of God," but it also sounds similar to the Hebrew word meaning "heard of God." Hannah recognized that her son was a direct gift from the Lord—that He had heard her prayer and had granted her request. She also did not forget her vow, and fulfilled it faithfully.

21. AND HIS VOW: Elkanah had the power to nullify his wife's vow according to God's law (Numbers 30:6–15), yet here we find that he knew of her vow and supported it fully. In God's eyes, Hannah's vow became binding on her husband as well, and Elkanah recognized his solemn responsibility to see that it was fulfilled. In this, he demonstrated his deep love for his wife far more than his words of encouragement could have done.

22. NOT UNTIL THE CHILD IS WEANED: Jewish custom at the time was to breast-feed a child until he was two or three years old.

REMAIN THERE FOREVER: Notice that Hannah did not say, "He will remain in the Lord's presence all his life." She understood that the Lord's children will be in His presence far beyond this earthly life, enjoying His company for all eternity.

24. THE CHILD WAS YOUNG: Samuel was probably around three years old when he entered the Lord's service at the temple.

28. I ALSO HAVE LENT HIM TO THE LORD: This does not mean that Hannah was permitting the Lord to borrow her son for a time, but that she was devoting him fully to the Lord's service with no expectation of receiving him back again.

⌁ READING 1 SAMUEL 2:1–21 ⌁

HANNAH'S SONG: *Hannah is so overjoyed at the Lord's miraculous answer to her request that she pours out her heart once again—this time in praise and joy.*

1. MY HEART REJOICES IN THE LORD: What a majestic contrast between this prayer and Hannah's earlier one! Here her heart was filled to overflowing once again—but this time with praise and adoration. Her prayer was actually a song, or psalm, of praise to the Lord's faithfulness and power, and it bears many similarities to the song that Mary sang upon receiving the news that she would bear the Son of God (Luke 1:46–55).

3. Let no arrogance come from your mouth: The Lord humbles those who raise themselves against Him, and raises those who humble themselves before His will. We see this in the contrasts between Samuel and Eli, two spiritual leaders in Israel, and between Saul and David, two very different kings. More importantly, we see a strong contrast between the attitudes of Hannah and Peninnah: Peninnah gloried in her fertility, as though she were responsible for her ability to bear children, while Hannah recognized that such things are from the Lord. Hannah took her sorrow and her heart's desire to the Lord, and those who submit themselves to God's sovereignty shall be blessed—while those who arrogantly follow their own will shall be humbled.

5. the barren has borne seven: Hannah gave birth to a total of six children (the *seven* here is poetic, not intended as prophecy). She asked the Lord for one child, and He poured out an abundance in reply. God loves to have His children turn to Him for all their needs, and He loves "to do exceedingly abundantly above all that we ask or think" (Ephesians 3:20). Peninnah became "feeble" by comparison; she may have born sons and daughters, but it was Hannah's son who became Israel's prophet and judge, the anointer of kings.

9. by strength no man shall prevail: Those who trust in their own power and wisdom shall be broken, but those who trust fully in the Lord shall find that He fights on their behalf. Again, we see this contrast in the lives of Samuel and David versus Eli and Saul. Hannah placed her faith in the Lord's power, and she was not disappointed.

18. wearing a linen ephod: Samuel apparently began to assist Eli in his duties as soon as he could walk and talk. The ephod was a sleeveless outer vest that extended to the hips, worn on top of the priest's tunic. Eli evidently had a miniature ephod made that would fit little Samuel.

19. his mother used to make him a little robe: This touching picture shows us that Hannah never stopped loving Samuel as her firstborn son. She continued to minister to his needs, and by doing so she also participated in his ministry before the Lord.

21. the Lord visited Hannah: Once again, we are reminded that life is a gift from God, and every conception is a direct result of His intervention. The Lord eventually blessed Hannah with six children: four sons and two daughters.

᚛ First Impressions ᚜

1. *Why did Peninnah abuse Hannah about her childlessness? What did this reveal about Peninnah's character? About Hannah's character? About their home life?*

2. Why did Eli think that Hannah was drunk? What does this reveal about Eli's character? About Hannah's grief?

3. In what ways did Hannah remain a good mother to Samuel? What did her sacrifice cost her? What did she gain?

4. In her song, how did Hannah describe God? List some of the surprising things the Lord does in this song?

⤳ Some Key Principles ⤶

God is the author of all life.

Hannah recognized that it was the Lord's responsibility to provide her with children, or to withhold them as He saw fit. Her childlessness caused her deep grief because people in her day generally viewed a lack of children as a sign of God's disapproval. This view in itself underscores the fact that it is God's choice to bestow children or to withhold them.

In modern times, we hear a lot about "choice" when it comes to children. Ironically, that "choice" is often a euphemism for abortion, the wanton slaying of a God-given life within a woman's womb. This idea, however, implies that human life is a choice made by a man or a woman—but the Scriptures are clear that life is given by God; the choice is His alone to make.

Children are a blessing from God, not a burden or a "lifestyle" choice. The married couple who gain a child have great cause for rejoicing, while the childless couple should pour out their request before the Lord as Hannah did. "Behold, children are a heritage from the LORD, the fruit of the womb is a reward. Like arrows in the hand of a warrior, so are the children of one's youth. Happy is the man who has his quiver full of them; they shall not be ashamed, but shall speak with their enemies in the gate" (Psalm 127:3–5).

This sovereignty over life does not stop merely at conception. Hannah sings that "the LORD kills and makes alive; He brings down to the grave and brings up" (1 Samuel 2:6). In the same way that God divinely and sovereignly causes pregnancy, He also is the one ultimately in control of how long people live. Beyond even that, Hannah describes the Lord as the one who not only determines life span but is sovereign over eternity as well. He is the one who sends people to the grave, as well as the one who brings people to everlasting life.

The Lord uses the weak things of the world for His glory.

Throughout history, God has routinely chosen the unexpected and unlikely to be recipients of His grace. He chose Abram and Sarai, who by all accounts were too old to have children, and promised that they would produce a nation. He chose Israel, who were weaker than all of their neighbors and in captivity, to become His people. And we already saw that He chose David, the youngest of his family, to be king over those people. This same way of working is seen in Hannah's life. She can declare from personal experience that the Lord is the one who blesses the needy and humbles the proud (1 Samuel 2:7–8).

63

This is the way God still works today. In His mysterious way, He "has chosen the foolish things of the world to shame the wise, and God has chosen the weak things of the world to shame the things which are mighty" (1 Corinthians 1:27). He does this to prove that there is not a human explanation behind the gospel; it must be entirely supernatural.

There were any number of Israelite wives whom God could have used to bring Samuel into the world. But God wanted a woman who was desperately dependent on Him. God had Hannah bring forth Samuel, and not Peninnah, because He gets more glory from being served by those who are absolutely dependent upon Him.

The Lord loves to have His children pour out their hearts to Him.

Hannah had suffered a great deal because of a situation that was beyond her control. It was not her fault that she had no children—such matters are in the hands of the Lord—but it caused her much heartache. To make matters far worse, she was constantly mocked and humiliated by her husband's other wife, Peninnah, who reminded her day after day of her barrenness. She bore the humiliation and sorrow until her heart reached the point that it must certainly have broken from the pain.

Then she found the solution. It was not some wonder drug that opened Hannah's womb; neither did she turn to the learning of science—indeed, she finally stopped turning to others for her answer, and turned instead to the Lord. She poured out her heart fully, without attempting to clothe her emotions in fancy prayers or stilted words. She told the Lord all her grief, poured out her ache and sorrow, and pleaded with Him for an answer—and the Lord was pleased with her prayer.

Our Father has not changed, and He still delights in the honest, open prayers of His children. He wants us to find all our answers in Him, telling Him our deepest desires and most private pains. And Jesus promised that God would answer the prayers of those who pray according to His will. He said, "Most assuredly, I say to you, whatever you ask the Father in My name He will give you. . . . Ask, and you will receive, that your joy may be full" (John 16:23–24). John later taught us that "if our heart does not condemn us, we have confidence toward God. And whatever we ask we receive from Him, because we keep His commandments and do those things that are pleasing in His sight" (1 John 3:21–22).

↳ Digging Deeper ↰

5. *Why did Hannah pour out her grief to the Lord? What result did she expect from her prayers? What does this reveal about God's character?*

6. *Why did Hannah promise to devote her son to the Lord's service? Why did the Lord wait until that moment to grant her request?*

7. *What does this passage reveal about God's role in childbearing? About a parent's role?*

8. How does Hannah's song describe God's sovereignty? How is Hannah's understanding of God's control different from how the world views God?

ᕙ Taking It Personally ᕗ

9. What promises have you made to the Lord? To other people? How well are you keeping those promises?

10. What principles in this passage tie in with the modern practice of abortion? How does the Lord view an "unwanted pregnancy"?

~ 7 ~
DAVID AND JONATHAN

↜ CHARACTERS' BACKGROUND ↝

In this study, we will fast-forward to the reign of Saul. The near-mad king was still holding the throne in Israel, but David had already been anointed as God's chosen king. This situation was naturally bringing a degree of conflict—a nation cannot have two kings, and one of the two men would have to go. Saul, therefore, set about getting rid of David in the vain hope that he could hold on to the kingship himself, passing it on to his son.

David, meanwhile, had been completely faithful to King Saul, serving him valiantly as a soldier. This, however, only served to increase the battle, as Saul became conflicted in his own mind about whether or not to murder the young man who had been so devoted. Saul began to slip into dangerous instability, one minute swearing loyalty to David, and the next minute throwing spears at his head.

Into this deadly situation stepped Jonathan, Saul's son and heir to the throne. Because David was Jonathan's main rival to the throne, one would expect Jonathan to take matters into his own hands, killing David himself. Jonathan was an important leader in Israel's army, a fighting man with great power and skill, and he would be king, as long as David was not around. But that is not what Jonathan chose to do; Jonathan knew that the Lord had chosen David to be king, not him. So instead of joining Saul in eliminating David, he opted to remain loyal to his closest friend. These two great men of valor shared a deep love for God, and that forged their devotion to each other.

↜ READING 1 SAMUEL 20:1–42 ↝

DAVID SEEKS A FRIEND: *David has been hiding from Saul, who is intent upon killing him, but now he turns to his closest friend for help: Saul's son Jonathan.*

1. DAVID FLED: Saul had determined to murder David, and had already tried to pin him against the wall with his spear, so David had fled to Samuel. Saul sent men after him, but the Spirit of the Lord prevented them from capturing him. After a time, David took flight again to avoid Saul's men.

Jonathan: Jonathan was the son of Saul, and heir to the throne in Saul's mind. (The Israelites had already started to follow the ways of the world by assuming that a king's son would become king in the future—which was not the Lord's plan.)

What is my iniquity: David had done nothing to provoke Saul—on the contrary, he had done many things in loyal service. He had already slain Goliath and had subsequently led very successful raiding parties against the Philistines. He was also the only person in Saul's court who could soothe the king's troubled spirits with his music. But Saul was still intent upon killing him, because David was the Lord's anointed king. Saul was losing his sanity in his determination to cling to power.

2. It is not so: At this point, Jonathan was evidently unaware of Saul's intentions to murder David, and apparently did not know that Saul had already thrown his spear at him. Saul had also sworn an oath to not kill David, and Jonathan fully trusted his father's word. In fact, his relationship with Saul appears to have been quite close, as he fully expected his father to take him into his confidence on matters of state. Jonathan's friendship with David had grown very strong, but this situation threatened to put him in a very difficult position. If his father was in fact trying to kill David, Jonathan would have to choose where his deepest loyalties lay.

3. Your father certainly knows: The friendship between Jonathan and David added fuel to Saul's determination to kill David, the young man he viewed as his rival for the throne. This also added to Jonathan's difficult predicament: he loved his father dearly and was completely loyal to him to the very day of their tragic deaths in battle. But he was also loyal to his friend David and recognized that David was the legitimate heir to the throne because he had been anointed by God.

4. Whatever you yourself desire: Jonathan had a healthy respect for those who had been anointed of God. He recognized that his final loyalty was to the Lord, not to any man—whether his father or his closest friend. David was God's anointed king, and Jonathan recognized his kingly authority.

A Covenant of Friendship: *David and Jonathan swear an oath together of love and faithfulness. Both men would keep the oath until their dying day.*

5. the New Moon: The Israelites held a sacrificial meal on the first day of each month as a way of consecrating the month to the Lord. Saul, as king, would have rightfully expected David to be present at the meal.

7. IF HE IS VERY ANGRY: Saul's response would reveal the truth in his heart. If he cared for David, he would be happy to have him be with his family for their annual gathering. But if he was consumed by envy—as he was—then he would become angry at David's absence. Saul wanted to know where David was at all times in order to kill him when the opportunity arose.

8. COVENANT: David and Jonathan had made a covenant of friendship (1 Samuel 18:1–3), and each loved the other like a brother. Both men would remain true to their word throughout their lives—David would even hold faithful to it many years after Jonathan's death. It is also important to recognize that Jonathan swore this oath to David before any trouble arose between David and Saul, yet Jonathan kept his word even after it became very costly to do so.

12. THE LORD GOD OF ISRAEL IS WITNESS: Here again we see the importance of keeping one's word. When a Christian commits to some course of action, he has made a commitment before the Lord.

SEND TO YOU AND TELL YOU: If Jonathan had good news for David, he would send a messenger to bring him back to court. But if it was bad news, Jonathan would go himself to tell David, sending him away from court.

14. THAT I MAY NOT DIE: Jonathan recognized that David would take the throne sooner or later, because the Lord had already anointed him king. It was customary in those days for a new king to put to death any member of a previous king's family to ensure that nobody could lay claim to the throne. Jonathan was asking David to not take such a step toward the family of Saul.

15. YOU SHALL NOT CUT OFF YOUR KINDNESS FROM MY HOUSE FOREVER: Jonathan may have suspected that he would not be alive when David took the throne, which indeed was the case, so he asked for mercy on his descendants as well. One day, David would keep his promise, showing great kindness to Jonathan's son Mephibosheth, who was lame (2 Samuel 9).

WHEN THE LORD HAS CUT OFF EVERY ONE OF THE ENEMIES OF DAVID: Jonathan was a man of great faith and loyalty. He knew that the Lord had chosen David, and he fully anticipated that David would become king and be established in Israel forever. There was no doubt in his mind that God's word would come to pass completely.

17. HE LOVED HIM AS HE LOVED HIS OWN SOUL: The friendship between Jonathan and David is an excellent model of the love that believers are to have toward one another. Each man was willing to sacrifice himself to protect the other, as Jonathan's actions would soon prove. Each man loved the other as he loved himself, as we are commanded to do in Matthew 22:39.

HATCHING THE PLAN: *Jonathan establishes a secret code by which he will tell David whether or not his life is in danger. He then returns to Saul's court to find out.*

19. THE PLACE WHERE YOU HID ON THE DAY OF THE DEED: This may refer to the place where David hid when he first fled from Saul (1 Samuel 19:2).

20. I WILL SHOOT THREE ARROWS: Jonathan's elaborate way of communicating the news to David was necessary if he was to keep David's location a secret. He could not even trust his own servants, lest Saul learn where David was hiding.

22. THE LORD HAS SENT YOU AWAY: Jonathan once again revealed his complete faith in the Lord's sovereignty. He viewed David's entire plight as part of God's plan.

26. HE IS UNCLEAN: Saul noticed David's absence immediately, but he initially assumed that he was ritually unclean, unable to participate in the worship feast (Leviticus 7:20–21).

28. DAVID EARNESTLY ASKED PERMISSION OF ME TO GO TO BETHLEHEM: We can assume that David spent the three days in Bethlehem with his family.

31. YOU SHALL NOT BE ESTABLISHED: Here we see a stark contrast between Jonathan and his father. Saul's chief concern was for his own political power, and he was outraged to discover that Jonathan did not share that priority. As long as David was alive, Jonathan's succession to the throne was in jeopardy, and Saul's line would die with him—but Jonathan's heart was fixed on obeying God, even though it meant he would never become king.

33. SAUL CAST A SPEAR AT HIM TO KILL HIM: Saul's self-will was slowly driving him to insanity, and his anger was consuming him—to the point that he was willing to murder his own son in a fit of rage in order to cling to his power. At this moment, Jonathan's eyes were opened to his father's true nature, and his conflict of loyalties was made clear.

38. MAKE HASTE, HURRY, DO NOT DELAY: As promised, Jonathan gave David the signal that he should leave the area and hide from Saul—but he added the loud proclamation that he must hurry, for his life was in imminent danger.

39. THE LAD DID NOT KNOW ANYTHING: Jonathan's caution proved very wise, as he discovered for himself. Saul would stop at nothing to find David, and it might have been disastrous to permit a servant lad to know of Jonathan's communications.

41. THEY WEPT TOGETHER: Both Jonathan and David were very masculine men, seasoned warriors and great leaders, yet they were not ashamed to display their masculine affection for one another with tears at their parting. This scene is deeply poignant, for it is unlikely that the two friends were ever together again.

↪ First Impressions ↩

1. Why was Saul trying to kill David? Why did Jonathan defend him?

2. Why did Jonathan make such an elaborate ruse to find out whether Saul intended to kill David? What does this reveal about the danger that Jonathan faced?

3. If you had been in Jonathan's place, how would you have handled this difficult situation? In David's place? In Saul's place?

4. Why did David and Jonathan become such committed friends? What might have been the foundation of their friendship?

↫ Some Key Principles ↬

The Lord is pleased with those who are faithful.

Jonathan and David were men of loyalty and faithfulness. Jonathan was loyal to his father, both as father and as king, and he was also loyal to David as friend and as the future king. Both he and David were completely faithful to their word, and David kept his vow of friendship long after Jonathan had died.

Such faithfulness can often come with a cost. Jonathan was caught in a very difficult situation where his loyalty to father and friend were in conflict. David's faithfulness to the Lord's anointed prevented him from doing any harm to Saul, even though Saul was actively trying to kill him. (We will look at this more closely in a later study.) For Jonathan, the cost of his faithfulness was the throne; as long as David was alive, Jonathan would never be king. The Scriptures are full of men and women who made faithfulness to God their highest priority, even at the cost of their own lives.

Hebrews 11 is filled with many heroes of the faith, men and women who placed their faith in God's word and demonstrated faithfulness to Him throughout their lives. Many "were tortured, not accepting deliverance, that they might obtain a better resurrection. Still others had trial of mockings and scourgings, yes, and of chains and imprisonment. They were stoned, they were sawn in two, were tempted, were slain with the sword. They wandered about in sheepskins and goatskins, being destitute, afflicted, tormented." And what does the Bible say of them? They are those "of whom the world was not worthy" (Hebrews 11:35–38). The Lord is pleased with those who remain faithful to Him.

God does not promise long life or material prosperity.

Jonathan was a man after God's own heart, just as David was—yet both men suffered injustice and hardship. Jonathan died young in battle, dutifully standing by his father the king. David had been anointed by Samuel to take the throne of Israel, yet he was forced to run for his life for many years. He hid in caves, lived with Israel's enemies, even feigned madness once in order to save his own life—yet he was faithful to the word of God.

The Lord does not promise His people that they will be exempt from suffering or hardship or sorrows—in fact, quite the opposite is true: those who follow Christ must expect to share in His sorrows, just as we share in His glory. David and other saints of Scripture understood this principle, so they did not lose heart when suffering came their way. Paul, for example, spent many years in various Roman prisons, even though his deep desire was to be traveling the world as a missionary. Yet his imprisonment led to a large portion of our New Testament.

God's people must not lose heart when suffering comes, for the Lord uses all things in our lives—both good and bad—to perfect His character in us. "My brethren, count it all joy when you fall into various trials, knowing that the testing of your faith produces patience. But let patience have its perfect work, that you may be perfect and complete, lacking nothing" (James 1:2–4).

Devotion to God outweighs the riches of the world.

Jonathan was the son of a king, and that position of honor brought with it many aspects of power and wealth. From the world's eyes, he was heir to the throne of Israel, and the entire army was at his command to protect that inheritance. His father, in fact, was actively working to remove Jonathan's sole "rival" to the throne, and all Jonathan needed to do was cooperate with Saul's plan to kill David, and his inheritance would have been (in Saul's thinking) fully secure.

But Jonathan cared nothing for the world's temporary advancements and fading glories. He understood that earth's kingdoms will all pass away, and only love shall remain—and he invested his future in his love for David. He was willing to sacrifice all the great honors that were his by birth, and he even risked his life in order to help David ascend the very throne that might have been his own. Saul chose to love his own legacy (and even his son) more than God. Jonathan esteemed the Lord's choice for king far ahead of his own interests.

Jesus says, "If anyone comes to Me and does not hate his father and mother, wife and children, brothers and sisters, yes, and his own life also, he cannot be My disciple"

(Luke 14:26). Christians are called to choose faithfulness to God over their own desires, and even over their families. This was a decision that Saul was not willing to make, and one that both Jonathan and David made gladly, knowing that the glories of serving God outweigh anything this world has to offer.

ᯇ Digging Deeper ᯇ

5. *In what ways was Jonathan's friendship to David very costly to himself? What does this reveal about his character?*

6. *Why did David and Jonathan make a covenant of friendship? On what was this covenant based? What pressures and situations were threatening their friendship?*

7.   What does it mean that Jonathan loved David "as he loved his own soul"? How would such a love be demonstrated, in practical terms?

8.   Even in their friendship, David and Jonathan loved God more than each other. How did they demonstrate this? Give some examples from their words and deeds.

9. In what areas of life do you find yourself putting your own interests above those of others? How do your friendships show the supremecy of God, as David and Jonathan's did?

10. What areas of faithfulness need strengthening in your own life? What commitments do you need to honor this week?

~ 8 ~
ELI AND HIS SONS

↶ HISTORICAL BACKGROUND ↷

We now return to the temple when Samuel was a young man, long before David had been anointed as king. As this study begins, Eli is still serving as high priest, and his two sons—Hophni and Phinehas—are priests under his authority. Eli is an old man, nearing the end of his life, and he has been serving in the temple for forty years.

After a lifetime of devoted service to the Lord one might expect Eli to have a close relationship with God and to be satisfied with life. But on the contrary a prophet comes to Eli with a dire message of coming judgment from God. Eli's compromises have finally caught up with him.

In this study, we will look at Eli's life and consider what led to such a tragic end. We will also consider his two sons, whose wicked behavior reflects his own failures. The message of Eli's tragic life is that doing the "right things" and being in the "right places" does not guarantee that a person is right with God. The Lord wants us to be obedient to His word in all areas of our lives, and He is more concerned with that than with our outward displays of service.

↶ READING 1 SAMUEL 2:12–36 ↷

ELI'S SONS: *Eli's two sons, Hophni and Phinehas, work as priests in the temple of the Lord. They are wicked men who abuse their authority and mistreat the people.*

12. THEY DID NOT KNOW THE LORD: This is perhaps the saddest indictment of Eli, the man who served the nation of Israel as their high priest yet failed to teach his own sons about the Lord. Interestingly, we discovered the same situation in Samuel's life— yet the two men's lives were very different. The problem in Eli's life was that he himself did not seem to know the Lord, or at least to recognize His presence. He had failed to introduce Samuel, as well as his sons, to the Lord, and he assumed that Hannah was drunk when she knelt pouring out her heart to God. The chief difference between Eli and Samuel is that Samuel walked closely with God, while Eli did not.

13–15. THE PRIESTS' CUSTOM WITH THE PEOPLE: Eli's sons were not following the Law regarding which portions of an offering were for their own use. The Law stipulated that the priests were entitled to certain specific parts of a sacrificed animal (Leviticus 7:34; Deuteronomy 18:3), while the rest belonged to the Lord—but Eli's sons were grasping at random. They were also required to sacrifice the fat portions to the Lord first, but the priests were taking their own share first rather than offering the first part to God.

16. THEY SHOULD REALLY BURN THE FAT FIRST: The people themselves understood the requirements of the Law better than Eli's sons did. It is a great tragedy when the Lord's anointed spiritual leaders care less for God's Word than an ordinary layperson. Eli's sons were treating God's commands with contempt.

I WILL TAKE IT BY FORCE: The priests received portions of certain offerings only by the free will of the people, not by force or coercion. Eli's sons were taking the meat as though it were theirs by right, when in fact it was up to the people making the offering to bring extra to the priests (Leviticus 7:28–36).

17. MEN ABHORRED THE OFFERING OF THE LORD: This is a profound statement—notice that it does not say "the young men," meaning Eli's sons, but "men" in general abhorred the offering of the Lord. In other words, the wicked actions of Eli's sons caused many others to treat God's worship with contempt.

ELI SLAPS THEIR WRISTS: *Eli has a responsibility to remove his sons from their positions, because he is the high priest. But he fails to do so.*

22. HE HEARD EVERYTHING HIS SONS DID: Eli was not directly to blame for the sins his sons committed, but he *was* fully responsible for their actions as priests, since he was the high priest.

THEY LAY WITH THE WOMEN: The women would have been serving the Lord in some voluntary capacity (Exodus 38:8), much as Hannah did when she came annually to visit Samuel. The sons of Eli were abusing their authority by coercing women into sexual immorality, probably by some form of threats similar to the way they obtained meat offerings (v. 16). The pagans in Canaan served a variety of fertility cults, most of which included temple prostitution, and Eli's sons were imitating the culture of the world around them by incorporating worldly practices into God's worship—to say nothing of their own immoral behavior.

23. WHY DO YOU DO SUCH THINGS? : Eli's response to his sons was grossly inadequate. His lenience as an overindulgent parent is not the issue here—it is his solemn responsibility as high priest. His sons were disqualified to be priests by their personal immorality, and they were also desecrating the Lord's temple with their evil practices. Either of those reasons was sufficient to remove them from their priestly offices, and Eli was obligated to do so both for the protection of the people and for the sanctity of God's temple. This little confrontation with his sons was insufficient, and the Lord held him accountable for not actively restraining his sons (1 Samuel 3:13). Eli's great failure was in not holding the things of God in reverence.

25. IF A MAN SINS AGAINST THE LORD, WHO WILL INTERCEDE FOR HIM? : This rhetorical question is a cause both for terror and for rejoicing. It was a terrifying warning to Eli's sons because they were sinning against God Himself when they treated His worship with contempt—for God was then both the injured party and the judge. On the other hand, it is a cause for rejoicing to Christians, for the answer to the question is Jesus! "My little children, these things I write to you, so that you may not sin. And if anyone sins, we have an Advocate with the Father, Jesus Christ the righteous. And He Himself is the propitiation for our sins, and not for ours only but also for the whole world" (1 John 2:1–2).

THE LORD'S PROPHECY OF JUDGMENT: *A prophet comes to Eli and declares that the Lord will bring judgment upon his house, because he has caused Israel to sin.*

THE LORD DESIRED TO KILL THEM: This does not mean that Eli's sons had no choice but to sin because God forced them to, in order to kill them. It means, rather, that they had stubbornly persisted in their sins for so long that their opportunity for repentance had passed. They had made a firm decision, hardening their hearts against the Lord, and their time of judgment was at hand.

27. THE HOUSE OF YOUR FATHER: That is, Aaron, Moses' brother, the first man chosen by God to be high priest over Israel and the man through whom all future priests would come.

28. TO OFFER UPON MY ALTAR: The Lord summarized the functions of a priest as three things: (1) making offerings; (2) burning incense; (3) wearing the ephod (a priestly garment). These things are symbolic of the three responsibilities of God's people: confessing sins; worshipping God; living righteous lives. Eli had failed in all these areas during his service before the Lord.

ALL THE OFFERINGS: The Lord further confronted Eli with the question, "Didn't you have enough to eat in the offerings that I had already provided? Why did you need to take those things that were not yours to take?" Notice that the Lord was confronting Eli with his sons' actions, *as though they were his own* sins. In effect, the sins of the priests under Eli's leadership became the sins of Eli—he was accountable for them, because he did not correct them.

79

29. **HONOR YOUR SONS MORE THAN ME:** Eli's sin essentially is this: he honored his sons more than he honored God. He elevated his idea of what was best for his sons over and above God's commands for holiness. When he permitted them to continue in their sin, he was effectively saying that his sons' self-satisfaction was more important than God's temple and His Law.

35. **A FAITHFUL PRIEST:** This prophecy was partially fulfilled in men such as Samuel and Zadok (1 Kings 1), and was ultimately completed in the person of Jesus Christ.

36. **BOW DOWN TO HIM FOR A ... MORSEL OF BREAD:** This judgment was fitting to Eli's sons, who had abused their authority to satisfy the lusts of the flesh. Future generations would be powerless to get more than a morsel of bread.

⤙ READING 1 SAMUEL 4:1–18 ⤚

THE FRUIT OF ELI'S SIN: *The Lord's judgment falls upon Eli and his sons as prophesied, but the results are more far-reaching still, as Israel loses the ark of the covenant.*

3. **LET US BRING THE ARK OF THE COVENANT:** The people of Israel clearly understood that the Lord was the one who fought their battles, and that a defeat indicated that something was wrong in their relationship with Him. What they did not understand, however, was that the ark of the covenant was not a magical good luck charm that would carry the presence of God wherever they chose. Their confusion and lack of understanding further underscores the fact that Eli had failed in his duties as high priest to teach the people the ways of the Lord.

5. **ALL ISRAEL SHOUTED:** This is a very sad picture, because the people of Israel thought they were placing their trust in the Lord's presence, when in fact they were merely trusting in a man-made object. It shows that the Israelites were willing to follow the ways of the Lord, if only the priests had been willing to lead them correctly. That the people were led so far astray by Eli and his wicked sons accentuates the magnitude of his failure as high priest.

7. **THE PHILISTINES WERE AFRAID:** This could have been a glorious day of victory for the Lord's people—if they had been truly following the Lord's leadership. Instead, it turned into a day of disgrace, bringing scorn on the name of the Lord because of Eli's poor shepherding.

18. **HE HAD JUDGED ISRAEL FORTY YEARS:** What a tragic end to a life of service! Yet Eli's service was more to himself than to the Lord, and his sons had taken that attitude to its logical conclusion by despising the things of God completely. Eli's life demonstrates

that a person can be outwardly involved in the service of God while truly being more concerned with service to self.

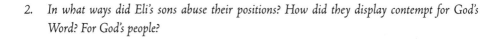 First Impressions ⌒

1. *How could a priest of the Lord not know the Lord (1 Samuel 2:12)? What led Eli's sons to that point?*

2. *In what ways did Eli's sons abuse their positions? How did they display contempt for God's Word? For God's people?*

3. *What did Eli do to address the sins of his sons? What did God want him to do?*

4. *If you had been in Eli's position, how would you have handled your sons' behavior?*

⤳ Some Key Principles ⤳

Our sin can lead others into sin.

The wicked deeds of Eli's sons were bad enough in themselves, more than sufficient to disqualify them for their roles as priests. But the more damaging aspect to their sins lay in the fact that they also led others into sin. They seduced women at the temple who had come there to serve the Lord, thereby turning their good intentions into wicked deeds.

Eli's failure to teach his sons about the ways of the Lord enabled them to treat God's Word with contempt. On a larger scale, his own disregard for God's Word led the entire nation into error. The people of Israel came to think that they could control the presence and power of God by using the ark of the covenant as a lucky charm, and this led to the terrible tragedy of losing the ark to the Philistines.

None of us lives in a vacuum, and our decisions and actions always affect those around us. This principle applies to godliness as well as to sin; we can influence others for good by obeying God's Word, or we can influence others for evil by disregarding His Word. We must guard against the attitude that some "small indulgence" will not harm anyone, for our actions have consequences that we cannot predict.

Serving the Lord effectively requires obedience to His Word.

Eli served the Lord at the temple for forty years, and even acted as one of Israel's last judges. He had risen to the highest level in the priestly class, achieving the greatest honor and responsibility a Levite could obtain. He had devoted nearly half his life to this high calling—yet in the end it was all in vain, and he died literally as a broken man.

Compare Eli to Samuel. He, too, devoted his entire life to the service of God—yet his life ended very differently from Eli's. The difference between the two men lies in their personal walk with God, not in their outward acts of service. Eli demonstrated that a person can devote himself to doing all the right things on the outside while still not knowing God in a saving way.

Knowing God is not an intellectual exercise; it is a spiritual devotion—it comes from submitting oneself to Him as Savior and obeying Him as Lord. Eli did not know God's voice because he had not lived in obedience to it. We must take care to not repeat his mistake. "You are My friends," Jesus said, "if you do whatever I command you" (John 15:14).

True religion is not seen in outward symbols.

The Israelites, or at least a great number of them, seemed to think that the ark possessed special powers. In some way, it seems, they thought that the Lord resided inside the ark of the covenant. They assumed that God lived in a box, and that if they brought that box into battle, then they would have success. Notice their response when they not only lost the battle but lost the ark as well: Eli died of shock, and the people acted as if they had lost their God.

The Lord used this entire event to punish his people for their sin, to show Eli's ignorance of His true nature, and to even bring a testimony of the greatness of the Lord over the Philistines' god, Dagon (1 Samuel 5). How silly it is to think not only that God resides in a box (or any other religious symbol), but that by losing that symbol the power of God is likewise lost. This thinking makes the Lord dependent on His people, rather than the other way around. And notice also how the Israelites tried to manipulate the Lord: they thought that, if they brought the ark, the Lord would have to give them victory. The Lord showed that He is not confined to a symbol, and that He—not the people—determines the outcome of the battle.

↤ Digging Deeper ↦

5.   When have you been called on to confront a loved one about sin? When has someone confronted you about sin in your life? How did you respond?

6.   What were the motives of the Israelites when they brought the ark into battle with them? What did the Lord teach them by having them lose both the battle and the ark?

7. Why did the Lord send such a stern judgment upon Eli's entire family? What does this reveal about God's character? About the seriousness of Eli's sins?

8. How can the loss of the ark of the covenant be traced back to Eli's failure as high priest? What does this demonstrate about the wide-ranging effects of sin?

ᴗ TAKING IT PERSONALLY ᴗ

9. What effect is your life having on people around you? Are you leading others toward godliness or toward sinfulness?

10. Is there an aspect of God's Word that you tend to ignore? What area of obedience might He be calling you toward in the coming week?

~ 9 ~
SAUL

1 SAMUEL 9–10; 28

ᴧ CHARACTER'S BACKGROUND ᴧ

We have already seen that Saul was Israel's first king, and it didn't take long to find that he was a failure, rejected by God. In this study, we will turn back to his youth and first appearance in Scripture, just prior to being anointed as king. We will discover a young man with vast potential: strong, handsome, standing head and shoulders taller than all his peers, a man with training and breeding, wealth and education. From the world's perspective, he had the perfect background and ideal preparation for a king.

And yet, when we fast-forward to Saul's last day of life, it does not compare favorably with his promising youth. We find a terrified man fraught with indecision, desperate for some wisdom from God—but willing to turn to the devil to find it.

What happened in between these two periods? What changed the young man of potential into a king whom God Himself discarded? The Lord had given Saul everything he *really* needed to be king, including His Holy Spirit, but Saul still failed. We will find that God may call us to a task, but it is up to us to obey—and Saul didn't.

ᴧ READING 1 SAMUEL 9:1–10:9 ᴧ

INTRODUCING YOUNG SAUL: *We now meet Saul when he is a young man, just prior to being anointed as Israel's first king. He has great potential, both for good and for failure.*

9:1. A MIGHTY MAN OF POWER: Saul's father was a wealthy and influential man. Saul was probably raised with all the advantages that the world had to offer. He was most likely well educated. His father had servants, so Saul had ample experience in commanding men. From the world's perspective, this young man had everything needed to become a great king. The Lord's perspective, however, is vastly different from that of the world.

2. A CHOICE AND HANDSOME SON: There are some interesting similarities and contrasts between the backgrounds of Saul and David. Both men were described as very handsome—although Saul was also very tall, standing head and shoulders above his peers, quite literally. We have seen already that the Lord does not look upon the outward appearance the way man does, and in Saul we will see why.

SAUL: The name *Saul* means "asked for." Saul was the king the people had asked for, and he lived up to all the dire warnings of Samuel (1 Samuel 8:11–18). The Lord would later select David, who proved to be the sort of king of God's choosing.

5. LET US RETURN: Saul would frequently give up following the Lord's commands when circumstances became difficult. This is one way in which Saul differed from David. While Saul gave up on his assignment without completing it, David would fight both a lion and a bear single-handed to serve his father and protect his sheep.

SEEKING THE LORD'S PROPHET: *Saul's servant informs him that a "seer" lives nearby, and suggests that they seek him out. The "seer," however, has more than donkeys in mind.*

6. THERE IS IN THIS CITY A MAN OF GOD: It would appear that Saul's ignorance of the ways of God extended to his earliest years. He needed his servant to tell him that Samuel, God's prophet and judge, lived in this city. The entire nation of Israel knew Samuel and where he lived, so it is not a good indication that Saul didn't even know who he was.

7. WHAT SHALL WE BRING THE MAN? : Saul was always concerned with outward appearances, with doing the socially correct thing—but not so concerned with doing what was right in God's eyes. It was common to offer a gift to a prophet in those days if one were asking for guidance of some kind. Saul was careful to obey social etiquette in offering a gift, but not so careful to obey what the prophet commanded him.

8. I HAVE . . . SILVER: Saul did not even provide his own gift for Samuel, but instead relied upon his servant's generosity—even though he was the son of a wealthy man. Saul was not a strong leader, as we find him in his earliest appearance following the leadership of his servants.

14. THERE WAS SAMUEL: This passage demonstrates once again the absolute sovereignty of God over the affairs of men, even to the little mundane affairs of daily life. The Lord used some wandering donkeys to lead Saul to Samuel in order to anoint him as king. Each step along the way could be viewed as simple coincidence, but there are no coincidences in God's eyes.

LITTLE IN HIS OWN EYES: *Saul is taken aback by Samuel's words of greeting. He thinks himself unfit to be king. Samuel anoints him just the same and gives him a feast.*

21. Why then do you speak like this to me? : At this time in his life, Saul was still "little in his own eyes," as Samuel would comment years later (1 Samuel 15:17). Yet, as we have seen, the seeds of his prideful stubbornness were already sown, even at this early date.

22. sit in the place of honor: Here is another contrast between Saul and David. Saul was anointed publicly, with great honor and celebration. He was seated in the place of honor among thirty guests, and was fed the choicest parts of meat. David, on the other hand, was anointed in secret, and then returned to his sheep.

10:6. the Spirit of the Lord will come upon you: There is a dire contrast between this empowering of the Holy Spirit and one that came later in Saul's life. On both occasions, Saul prophesied among the Lord's prophets, but the later event would accentuate Saul's disgrace, rather than his anointing as king (1 Samuel 19).

turned into another man: Perhaps the saddest part of Saul's story is that it did not need to turn out as it did. The Lord loves to transform people from selfish sinners into selfless saints, and Saul could have become Israel's greatest king. But over his lifetime, he made a habit of following his own will rather than the Lord's will, and habits are what define our character.

8. Seven days you shall wait: This was one of Samuel's first commands to Saul, at the beginning of his kingship, and it was the very command that he disobeyed when he later offered sacrifices to the Lord rather than waiting for Samuel (see Study 4).

9. God gave him another heart: Saul began his kingship with the one thing he needed to defend Israel: the empowering of the Holy Spirit. Yet even this did not guarantee that he would walk faithfully with the Lord, because he did not know God in a saving way.

↳ Reading 1 Samuel 28:1–20 ↰

The Last Days of King Saul: *By the end of his life, the young man who was once little in his own eyes has grown old in stubborn self-will. Let us now fast-forward to look at the last day of his life. Saul was in yet another battle with the Philistines, and he was outnumbered, surrounded, and very desperate.*

1. in those days: We are now very near Saul's tragic end.

Achish: David had fled to the Philistine city of Gath, which was ruled by Achish. This put him in a very delicate situation, as the Philistines fully expected him to fight on their behalf against the army of Israel.

3. Saul had put the mediums and the spiritists out of the land: In Israel, those who practiced the occult arts were to be put to death (Leviticus 20:27). God hates witchcraft in any form, because the occult is the realm of Satan, and those who dabble in it are making themselves available to the devil and his minions. Saul had understood this, and had obeyed the Word of God—to a point. As we will soon see, his own self-interests always trumped God's Word.

5. he was afraid: Once again we find a stark contrast between Saul and David. Saul stood at the front of his entire army, whereas David had stood alone against Goliath. David was a man of courage (as we will see in Study 11), while Saul was a man of timidity. The difference between the two lay not in some character trait of courageousness, but in their respective views of God. Saul's final authority was his own will and expedience, and therefore his trust was in his own might. He had good reason to be afraid, if that was where his strength lay. David's strength, however, was in the Lord, and the Lord delivered him from all his enemies. This battle was to be Saul's last.

6. the Lord did not answer him: What a terrible ending, after such a promising beginning. The man who had been anointed by God and transformed into a prophet finished his days frightened and alone. The Lord had once inhabited Saul through His Holy Spirit, but now He would not even answer his call.

Saul and the Witch: *Saul's last act as king is to consult a medium, thus turning his back fully on the Lord. Both, ironically, are terrified when Samuel actually appears.*

7. Find me a woman who is a medium: In his moment of crisis, Saul revealed his true heart. He had previously obeyed the Lord's commands outwardly by removing witches from Israel, but his heart was still devoted to serving himself. Now he demonstrated that he held the Lord's commands in contempt, being willing to turn away from God and toward the devil in order to meet his own needs. It is also interesting to notice that Saul's servant knew exactly where to find such a person, even after witchcraft had been outlawed in Israel.

8. Saul disguised himself: Saul found himself in a snare of his own making. He had personally banned witches from the land, yet he now was seeking their service. In order to accomplish this, he decided to dress up, and hope that the witch would not see who he really was.

10. Saul swore to her by the Lord: The hypocrisy of this oath was breathtaking. Saul had completely abandoned any pretense of obeying the commands of the Lord, and had deliberately turned to demonic sources for guidance—yet he persisted in his outward appearances of godliness by invoking the Lord in his oath.

12. SHE CRIED OUT WITH A LOUD VOICE: There is a certain bitter humor in this picture. The witch did not expect to have a real human spirit appear before her, because her craft was drawn from the powers of hell, not the power of eternity. Mediums cannot talk with "departed spirits"; they can only connect with the unseen and fallen spirit beings that follow the devil. This witch may also have been a charlatan who was accustomed to deceiving her customers with phony mumbo jumbo, as many do today. Either way, she did not expect Samuel himself to appear before her.

15. WHY HAVE YOU DISTURBED ME: It is very important to recognize that mankind cannot contact those who have died. There are people who claim to do so, but those people are either outright frauds or (much worse) holding communication with demons. In this one case, however, it appears that the Lord permitted the spirit of Samuel to appear before Saul. There is no other event like this anywhere in Scripture.

I AM DEEPLY DISTRESSED: This was always Saul's excuse for disobeying the Word of God. Yet he himself had caused much deep distress in the life of David, and David had still remained faithful to God. The difference lay within the will of each man—it is not enough to perform an outward display of religion; we must also set our wills and our hearts to obedience, even when we are "deeply distressed."

16. THE LORD HAS . . . BECOME YOUR ENEMY: There can be no words more terrifying than these. If the Lord turns His back on a person, there is no further recourse—no source of mercy, truth, or life itself.

↤ FIRST IMPRESSIONS ↦

1. *Why did Saul balk at Samuel's desire to anoint him king? How did his attitude change over time? Why?*

2.   How did Saul differ from Samuel? From David? What was the chief reason for these differences?

3.   How might Saul have made a great king? What caused his failure?

4.   Why did Saul feel he needed to consult a witch? What would it have taken to restore his relationship with the Lord?

ᴗ Some Key Principles ᴗ

God uses even wicked people for His purposes.

Saul did not apply to be king. He was not lobbying for the job. The Lord chose him for it, and He did so because He wanted to give Israel what they deserved. The Israelites wanted a king so that they could be like the other nations, so God chose Saul, a king who was just like the other nations' kings. At the beginning of his reign, the Holy Spirit empowered Saul, and Israel was victorious. But when Saul chose to love himself rather than the Lord, the Spirit left him. From that moment on, the only victories Israel had were under David's leadership, and Saul's jealousy grew.

By the end of Saul's life, Israel was being decimated by their enemies, and Saul's ego had placed his own pride above Israel's well-being. In short, Israel was getting exactly what they asked for, and exactly what they deserved. The Lord used a sinful and uncooperative Saul to bring about the judgment that He wanted to execute on His own people. Saul spent his life fighting against the Lord's purposes, but in the end, his whole life was in fact spent fulfilling those very same purposes.

This same dynamic is seen in the death of Jesus. His biggest enemies—Judas, Pilate, and the Pharisees—all committed the greatest sin imaginable by crucifying the Son of God. And yet it was that sinful act that brought about God's plan of salvation for His children. Even the wicked are used by the Lord for His own purposes.

Sin produces self-deception.

The ironies in Saul's encounter with the witch are numerous. Saul had banned witches from the land, but then felt that he needed to use one. Saul had to wear a disguise so the witch would not fear legal punishment for using her practice when it was prohibited by the king himself. The whole incident begs the question, if Saul thought the witch had actual insight, did he not fear that she might also see through the disguise? The final ironic twist is seen in the witch's surprise when Samuel responded. It is clear that this was the first time she was ever actually successful.

All of these ironies show how self-deceived both Saul and the witch were. She knew her practice was a hoax, but she persisted in it anyway. Saul knew witches had no real power, but went to one for guidance anyway. Finally, Saul explained away his obvious disobedience by saying that the Lord would not answer his prayers, so that is why he needed Samuel, or at least a witch. Yet Samuel saw through that self-deception, and told Saul that the issue was his sin, not the Lord's punishment. As long as Saul was God's enemy, he would receive no answer to his prayers.

Saul was so self-deceived that, even after seeing Samuel and receiving the prophecy that he would lose the battle and die that day, he refused to repent. The witch brought him his last meal, and he returned to the battle—as blinded by sin as he was when he put on his disguise to begin with.

If we make a habit of obeying the Lord, it will be easier to obey in stressful times.

Saul was very concerned with outward appearances, and he took great care to say and do the "right things." He fretted about having a suitable gift for the seer when he couldn't find his donkeys, and later he made a great show of defeating the Amalekites and bringing home King Agag in triumph. The problem was that he was not supposed to keep Agag alive, and the Lord had expressly commanded him in that regard. Earlier in his life, Saul was concerned about the *etiquette* of dealing with God's prophet but not about the *obedience* that came with it.

Samuel, in contrast, had made it an overriding, lifelong habit to obey the Lord's voice. He learned that lesson as a boy in the temple, and he practiced it for the rest of his life. The Lord later commanded him to anoint David as king, and Samuel obeyed—despite the fact that he was risking his life in the process. Samuel obeyed the Lord in difficult circumstances because it was his habit, a habit developed on a daily basis.

We make something a habit by doing it frequently over an extended period of time. Physical exercise can become a habit if we do it each day for a few weeks. Obedience to God's Word can also become a habit, simply by the routine of obeying on a daily basis.

⤙ DIGGING DEEPER ⤚

5. *What does it mean that God made Saul a "new man"? What changed in him? Why didn't it make him a good king?*

6. Why did God refuse to answer Saul's prayers at the end of his life? What does this teach about prayer?

7. What was Saul's response to Samuel's dire warning? Is this what you expected from him? How is it in keeping with his character?

8. How do you see hypocrisy and self-deception in this section? Give some examples.

⌒ Taking It Personally ⌒

9. Which habit is strongest in your daily life: the habit of obedience or the habits of indulgence? What area of obedience could you strengthen this week?

10. What gifts has God given you? How are you using those gifts to obey Him more fully?

Section 3:

Themes

In This Section:

～ 10 ～

RESPECTING GOD'S KING

⤝ THEMATIC BACKGROUND ⤞

As our passage opens, Saul had been hunting David in hopes of murdering him for some time, and David had been hiding anywhere he could. David had also assembled a small group of fighting men who accompanied him, some four hundred men who had left Israel for their own reasons. David had already led that fighting band against the Philistines, and the Lord had given him great success.

But nothing David did would alleviate Saul's hatred, and the king pursued him day after day throughout the wilderness in hopes of putting him to death once and for all. This was very taxing on David, to say the least, and on his men as well. They were forced to live in caves and woodlands, foraging for supplies and constantly on the run from one place to the next. They could not remain in any place for long, because even the Israelites themselves might betray them to Saul.

Then one day, when David and his men were hiding in a cave, the Lord delivered Saul into his hand. David was given the perfect opportunity to end this madness once and for all. After all, wasn't he already anointed king of Israel? If anyone had the right to slay an attacker, it was the persecuted and legitimate king of Israel. But David stayed his hand and refused to do any harm to Saul, because he was intent upon respecting the one whom the Lord had anointed as king.

⤝ READING 1 SAMUEL 24:1–22 ⤞

SAUL HUNTS DAVID: *Saul takes some time off from fighting the Philistines to pursue his obsession: trying to kill David.*

1. SAUL HAD RETURNED FROM FOLLOWING THE PHILISTINES: Saul's kingship was marked by constant fighting against the Philistines, and the nation of Israel knew very few times of peace during his reign. It was not until well into David's reign that the Philistine menace was quelled once and for all.

David is in the Wilderness of En Gedi: As important as the Philistine threat was to Saul, there was another priority that was higher still: killing David. Saul many times set aside whatever he was doing to pursue David, and this made David's life a constant anxiety, as he fled from one location to another just to stay alive.

2. David and his men: By this time, David had assembled a small fighting band of his own, composed of men who had their own reasons for fleeing Israel—most of them not very good reasons. He had gathered some four hundred men, "everyone who was in distress, everyone who was in debt, and everyone who was discontented" (1 Samuel 22:2). David's men were unskilled warriors (although they were becoming more skilled as time passed), while Saul went after them with "three thousand chosen men from all Israel"—three thousand elite troops chasing after four hundred untrained men. David was outnumbered and under-equipped.

Rocks of the Wild Goats: David was reduced to living in caves and atop wild crags, moving constantly to stay alive. He was the legitimate king of Israel, yet he lived as an outlaw in the most uncomfortable and perilous conditions.

Nature Calls: *Saul uses a cave to relieve himself, but does not realize that David is hiding inside. This is David's big chance to kill his enemy.*

3. Saul went in to attend to his needs: Saul had to relieve himself. The literal phrase is that Saul went into the cave to "cover his feet." He would have been crouching in a corner with his inner garment dropped to his feet. He was in a very vulnerable position—and David's fighters were hidden right nearby.

4. This is the day: Here we find David faced with a very difficult decision. The Lord had anointed David as king and Samuel had told him that he would rule Israel, so it must have seemed like divine providence that Saul should be delivered into his hand in this way. On the other hand, David knew that Saul had also been anointed by the Lord at one time. He had since been rejected as king, yet David recognized that it was not his place to raise his hand against the Lord's anointed—even when the anointed one had fallen away from God.

5. David's heart troubled him: David was so determined to respect the Lord's anointed king that he even felt guilty for cutting off a piece of Saul's robe—even when that piece of robe would prove that he had shown respect for Saul, winning him a season of peace. David recognized that the Lord had anointed Saul to be king, and it was the Lord's prerogative—and only His—to remove Saul from that position.

7. David restrained his servants: David was also anointed by the Lord to be king, and as such he took seriously his responsibility for those under his care. This concept cuts both ways: we are all called to respect those whom God has placed in authority over us, and we are also held accountable for those under our personal leadership. David recognized that if his men attacked Saul, he would be held accountable as well, since they were under his authority.

DAVID CONFRONTS SAUL: *David holds great respect for the Lord's anointed, but that does not mean that he pretends that evil is good. He confronts Saul with his sin.*

8. MY LORD THE KING: Notice the deep respect David showed to Saul, bowing himself to the ground and addressing him as "my lord." This was a remarkable way for David to respond to the man who was trying to murder him without any cause. David's words alone must have smitten Saul's conscience—especially when one considers that, had the tables been turned, Saul would not have hesitated to kill David.

10. THE LORD DELIVERED YOU TODAY INTO MY HAND: David's men saw the opportunity as the Lord's way of delivering Saul for David to kill, but David saw it as his opportunity to demonstrate humility and obedience to the Lord's will. Here is an example of the way David was a man after God's own heart, as he saw the events of life from the Lord's perspective rather than from that of the world.

11. THERE IS NEITHER EVIL NOR REBELLION IN MY HAND: From a legal perspective, perhaps David would have been justified in killing Saul when he had the opportunity, because Saul was actively trying to kill him. But David's view was that the Lord had allowed Saul to hunt him, and the Lord would be faithful to remove the threat when His time was right. In the meantime, David saw any armed resistance to Saul as an act of rebellion rather than simple self-defense. His defense was in the Lord, and he would not raise his hand against Saul.

12. LET THE LORD JUDGE BETWEEN YOU AND ME: Notice, however, that David did not gloss over the terrible deeds of Saul. He did not make believe that Saul was a good king or that he had some sort of divine right to murder David. His reason for not fighting back was that he wanted to be submissive to God's will, but he did not hesitate to ask the Lord to judge the wickedness he was enduring.

13. WICKEDNESS PROCEEDS FROM THE WICKED: This is as close as David came to rebuking Saul. He did not feel that it was his place to openly defy the king, but he also was willing to clearly state an important principle: our actions define our character. Those who act wickedly are wicked, but David would define his own character by not retaliating.

16. SAUL LIFTED UP HIS VOICE AND WEPT: Saul was confronted with his own wickedness simply by the contrast of David's righteousness.

22. David swore to Saul: Saul had sworn on more than one occasion that he would not kill David. Unlike Saul, however, David would keep his oath.

⌁ First Impressions ⌁

1. What suffering did David endure at the hands of Saul? How did he respond?

2. Explain why David did not kill Saul. What does this show about his understanding of God's control of Israel?

3. If you had been in David's situation with Saul in the cave, what would you have done? How would you have responded if you'd been in Saul's situation?

4.   *Why did David serve Saul as king, when David knew that he himself was the rightful king?*

⤳ Some Key Principles ⤳

Those who govern us are placed in authority by God.

Saul was not an effective king. As time went along, his grip on sanity became increasingly tenuous. What's worse, he was plagued by an evil spirit, subject to demonic attack and oppression. He was vastly unjust and was obsessed with trying to murder David—even though David had served him faithfully and selflessly.

Nevertheless, he was the king God had anointed over Israel, and all Israel was called to obey him and submit to his authority. The world would argue that David, at the very least, was exempt from this injunction. After all, he, too, was anointed king, and Saul was trying very hard to murder him. Wouldn't it have been acceptable for David to defy Saul's authority, as one peer to another? David's answer to that question was a resounding "no."

The world is not lacking in corrupt leaders and inept politicians, and some Christians around the world are faced with genuine, life-threatening persecution for their faith. But God's Word teaches us that believers are to submit themselves to the authorities the Lord has placed us under—even when those authorities are unjust. "Let every soul be subject to the governing authorities. For there is no authority except from God, and the authorities that exist are appointed by God. Therefore whoever resists the authority resists the ordinance of God, and those who resist will bring judgment on themselves" (Romans 13:1–2). The only exception to this rule is when an authority commands one to violate the law of God.

Do not revile those who persecute you.

David had been the only Israelite willing to stand up to Goliath, and he had wrought a great victory for Saul's army. He was the only person who could soothe Saul when the evil spirit persecuted him, playing music and singing psalms that he himself had probably written as a shepherd. Even after Saul had driven him out of his court, David continued to lead raids against the Philistines and to help Saul protect Israel against her enemies. Yet, in spite of all his faithful service, David suffered under a constant threat of murder, and was frequently betrayed by his own people.

If ever there was a person who had a right to speak harshly to his persecutor, it was David. But when he confronted Saul—even after sparing Saul's life when others wanted to kill him—David still did not revile his enemy. He respected Saul's position as king, and bowed with his face to the ground. He spoke the truth to Saul; he did not pretend that Saul was not sinning against him—but he spoke the truth in a humble fashion.

This can be a hard lesson to learn, but it is important if we are to be like Christ. The injustices against David pale to insignificance when compared with those heaped upon Jesus. The holy Son of God—who had never sinned, who created the heavens and earth—submitted Himself quietly to the scourging and mockery of His tormentors. "For to this you were called," the apostle Peter later taught, "because Christ also suffered for us, leaving us an example, that you should follow His steps: 'Who committed no sin, nor was deceit found in His mouth'; who, when He was reviled, did not revile in return; when He suffered, He did not threaten, but committed Himself to Him who judges righteously" (1 Peter 2:21–23).

Obedience does not always give deliverance.

David was in a dangerous situation. His king was hunting him with an elite unit of his army. David was forced to flee, and in so doing he lost his wife, his job, his position in the military, and any sense of peace. He went from being a national hero to being a criminal. He hid in caves, slept on rocks, and continually lived under the threat of death—and all this simply because the Lord had anointed him to be king.

David never wronged Saul. Moreover, David did not ask to be king. One has to wonder whether David might have preferred to be back in the field with his father's sheep rather than on the run. We could hardly blame him if he thought, *I wish that Samuel had chosen somebody else.* For nearly twenty years, David lived as a fugitive simply because he was being obedient to God.

There are many, especially in the contemporary charismatic movement, who teach that faithfulness brings health, wealth, and deliverance. David shows that the opposite is often true. For him, faithfulness brought persecution, homelessness, hunger, and rejection. In the Gospel of Matthew, Jesus told a scribe who wanted to follow Him, "Foxes have holes and birds of the air have nests, but the Son of Man has nowhere to lay His head" (Matthew 8:20). This is often the case with those who follow the Lord. Material things may diminish, but they are replaced by the peace of a right relationship with God, and the rewards of that outweigh anything the world has to offer.

ᴥ Digging Deeper ᴥ

5. *Why did God bring Saul into that particular cave where David was hiding? What was His purpose in this confrontation?*

6. *Why did David choose to not attack Saul? Were his men right or wrong for encouraging him to do so?*

7. *How do you respond to those who abuse their authority? How did David respond? How did Jesus respond?*

8. Why did God allow Saul to persecute David for so long? What was He teaching Saul? What was He teaching David? What was He teaching the nation of Israel?

↳ Taking It Personally ↲

9. Do you struggle with a rebellious spirit? In what areas might the Lord be calling you to be more submissive?

10. How have you responded recently to people who treat you badly? How can you imitate the humility of Christ this week?

～ II ～

COURAGE

～ THEMATIC BACKGROUND ～

The battle of David and Goliath is one of the best-known stories in the Bible—even people who have never read the Bible are familiar with the inexperienced teen who faced the seasoned giant. In fact, this story is often used as a sort of parable by the world to refer to anyone who challenges a stronger adversary. But this is not a mere fable; it is a literal account of an actual historical event—and the people involved were real human beings with real human emotions.

David was just a young man, probably still in his teens when he faced Goliath, and he experienced all the emotions and aspirations that any young man experiences—including fear. He was not a trained soldier, and he had never worn armor or hefted a shield in his life. Across the valley, however, there towered an immense giant, standing nearly ten feet tall and wielding superhuman weapons. How could a teenager be expected to charge into battle against such a foe?

We must remember that courage is not the absence of fear; it is the determination to act in faith, in spite of fear. Conversely, simply rushing forward into a fearful situation is not courage either; it is blindness or foolishness. True courage is drawn from the faith that God is sovereign, even in the face of adversity. David undoubtedly felt fear as he charged toward that terrible giant—but he kept charging just the same, because he knew that he was going not in his own strength but in the strength of the Lord. He alone is omnipotent, and He is faithful to fight for His people—just as He did for David.

The story of David and Goliath is primarily about God and His glory. Yet it also teaches us lessons about true courage, as we see David's faith tested in an extreme circumstance. But first we will look at his predecessor's *lack* of courage.

～ READING 1 SAMUEL 10:17–23 ～

SAUL HIDES IN THE BAGGAGE: *We begin by returning to the day when Saul was anointed king. He provides some contrast to the courage of young David.*

17. Samuel called the people together: This took place when Samuel anointed Saul as Israel's first king. We will see a distinct disparity here between Saul and David.

22. hidden among the equipment: Saul knew that he was going to be selected to serve as king, since Samuel had already told him of God's plan. His response to God's calling, however, was to run away and hide. On one hand, Saul's hiding among the supplies suggests a great humility, as though he felt completely unworthy and unequipped to be king—he was "little in his own eyes," as Samuel noted. In this, his view of himself was accurate. The problem was that he saw with his own eyes only, and lacked the Lord's perspective. The Lord saw him as a man of greatness, fit to become the sort of king that He desired. Saul never did learn to see the world through God's eyes in the way that David did, and the result was that what vision he did have became less and less accurate as time went along. What is more pertinent here is that Saul was focused only on his own strength, and he recognized (quite accurately) that he did not have the power in himself to become king. What he did not see, however, was that the Lord would give him the strength to perform what He had commanded him to do. If Saul had learned to look at God instead of himself, he would have found the courage he lacked.

⌁ Reading 1 Samuel 17:1–51 ⌁

The Philistines' Champion: *The armies of Israel and Philistia gather on opposite sides of a valley. Out of the Philistine ranks emerges a giant who defies the God of Israel.*

1. the Philistines gathered their armies: We now fast-forward to the time soon after David had been anointed as king in place of Saul. King Saul was busy with the task that occupied most of his life, fighting the Philistines. On this particular day, the Philistines had gathered in tremendous force to attack Israel, and Saul and his army were filled with fear.

4. six cubits and a span: Goliath was nearly ten feet tall! This story is not a fairy tale or folk legend; it is a literal historical event. There were other Philistine giants in David's day (archeologists have uncovered numerous giant skeletons), but Goliath was evidently a famed warrior who was idolized by the Philistines and feared by their enemies. A look at his equipment will reveal why.

5–6. bronze helmet . . . coat of mail . . . armor on his legs . . . bronze javelin: The ordinary Philistine soldier wore a leather helmet, and most of Israel's fighting men wore no helmets at all—but Goliath's helmet was of bronze. Goliath's coat of mail consisted of metal plates sewn atop a leather jacket, weighing approximately 125 pounds. Most of the Israelite fighters wore simple hide or leather tunics to protect their chests, with nothing on their lower torso—but Goliath even had metal armor on his legs. Most spears and javelins were made of wood, but his was made of bronze. His spear was so huge that it was the size of the wooden beam used to operate a weaver's loom. It was also equipped with an iron spearhead (only the Philistines had iron, much harder than bronze), the head alone weighing some fifteen pounds. Goliath was huge, and his weapons were terrifying.

IN SEARCH OF A MAN: *Goliath has issued a challenge to one-on-one combat, but not one man from Israel has stepped forward—including King Saul.*

8. CHOOSE A MAN FOR YOURSELVES: Goliath was challenging the Israelites to send out a champion of their own, and the two would fight one-on-one. This was not uncommon in David's day, as the two champions would decide the outcome of the battle rather than have the two armies engage. The underlying concept was that the two men would be stand-ins not just for their respective armies but for their respective gods. The result of the combat would reveal the will of the gods—and the relative strength of each god. Goliath, in effect, was claiming that his god was more powerful than Israel's God.

10. GIVE ME A MAN: The proper man to fight this battle was Saul. He was the king, and therefore he represented in his person the entire nation. He also was the tallest man in Israel, and was probably the closest physical match to Goliath—though still far removed from the Philistine's stature. Saul, however, was afraid, and did not fulfill his duty as king, because he was always looking on outward appearances, always focused on his own power. He failed in his courage because he failed in his focus.

DAVID ARRIVES: *Goliath continues to defy Israel's God for forty days, morning and night, without opposition. Then young David arrives on the scene.*

14. DAVID WAS THE YOUNGEST: This fact is pertinent for several reasons. First, we must remember that David was quite young when this battle took place, probably still in his teens. He was also the youngest in his family, which suggests that the responsibility for this battle would not fall on his shoulders. If it were up to the sons of Jesse to fight Goliath, it would have fallen to the firstborn son to do so. In many ways, David was a ridiculously unlikely opponent for this dreaded giant.

15. FEED HIS FATHER'S SHEEP: David had not set out that day looking for adventure, hoping to make a name for himself. He was merely doing the work that his father had given him to do. The Lord often brings opportunities for service into the lives of those who are focused on doing His work.

16. FORTY DAYS, MORNING AND EVENING: Goliath had been coming forth with his blasphemous defiance against the God of Israel twice a day, for more than a month. This situation was a disgrace to Israel's king.

20. THE ARMY WAS GOING OUT TO THE FIGHT: There is a certain irony in this statement, since there was no fight to join. One can picture the Israelite army drawn up across the valley from the Philistines, banging swords against shields, shouting taunts, clamoring for battle—but not fighting. Talk is easy, but fighting is costly. The Lord's army was indeed looking for a man, just as Goliath had claimed.

24. ALL THE MEN OF ISRAEL ... FLED FROM HIM: The moment a genuine foe arrived for battle, the bold Israelites melted away in fear. Once again we see the concern for outward appearances minus any concern for genuine obedience. The army, following Saul's example, made a grand display of courage, when in fact they had none. They had no courage because they had forgotten that the Lord is the one who fights His people's battles.

25. THE KING WILL ENRICH WITH GREAT RICHES: This offer reveals what motivated Saul. David was not motivated by such rewards.

26. TAKES AWAY THE REPROACH FROM ISRAEL: These are David's first recorded words in Scripture, and they reveal both his heart and his motivation. David was concerned with the fact that Israel's God was being profaned. It is remarkable that this young man who had never seen military combat was the only one to take umbrage on behalf of God—and he did so the moment he heard Goliath's first blasphemous taunt.

OPPOSITION FROM THE HOME TEAM: *David is ready and eager to face the terrible foe across the valley, but first he must face some opposition at home.*

28. ELIAB'S ANGER WAS AROUSED AGAINST DAVID: Eliab may have been jealous of his younger brother's preferment to king, or his conscience may have been smitten that the youngest was proving more courageous than he. The end result, however, was that a member of David's own family not only degraded David's courage, but in so doing tacitly condoned the degradation of the Lord.

32. LET NO MAN'S HEART FAIL BECAUSE OF HIM: Here stood David, a mere teenage shepherd, acting the role of military leader to the king himself! The king should have been encouraging the army, both by words and deeds, but he had long before failed in that role. Now a man of true courage—a man after God's own heart—was taking over.

35. I went out after it and struck it, and delivered the lamb from its mouth: Remember the picture of Saul wandering the countryside in search of his father's donkeys, then giving up and heading for home? In dramatic contrast, David had risked his own life and limb to save—not a whole flock of donkeys—but just one sheep. His great courage was motivated by a deep desire to be faithful to his father's work, and that commitment gave him courage to also face Goliath.

God Gives the Victory: *David drew his great courage from the Lord. He fully trusted that God would deliver him if he just took action—and he was not disappointed.*

37. He will deliver me from the hand of this Philistine: This is the foundation of David's great courage. His courage was in the Lord, not in his own fighting ability. Even if he had not fought lion or bear, he would still have come forward to fight against Goliath, because he was fully confident that the Lord would honor his obedience and provide the victory.

39. he had not tested them: There was nothing inherently wrong in bearing man-made arms and armor into battle; David would do so himself as he grew to manhood. But his focus was not on the weapons but on His God. He did not know how to use sword and shield, so he was quick to abandon them for the tools with which he was familiar. The weapons made no difference, since it was the hand of God that would be wielding them.

42. he disdained him: Those who look only upon outer appearances will be quick to despise the people of God, for they cannot see the power of the One who watches over them. Goliath's faith was in his own power and weapons, and David's weapons were laughable by comparison. But Goliath would not be laughing for long.

45. I come to you in the name of the Lord of hosts: David was fighting for the honor of God's name, which Goliath had defied and slandered day after day. David was absolutely convinced that the Lord would honor His commitment to His people, and that is what gave him the courage to step onto the field of battle. The Lord, who rules heaven, would not let Israel be defeated by someone like Goliath who openly mocked Him.

46. that all the earth may know that there is a God in Israel: Day after day, the army of Israel had stood across the valley and shouted similar threats at the Philistines, but David's threat was quite different. He had come forth to fight for the glory of God, to demonstrate to both Israelite and Philistine that the God of Israel was the only true God. He was fighting not for his own glory or the reward of Saul but for the name of God.

∽ First Impressions ∼

1. Why did Saul hide in the equipment when he was to be anointed king? What motivated him: cowardice? humility? confusion?

2. What motivated David to face Goliath? Why was his response to Goliath so different from Saul's?

3. Why did David's brother become angry with David's interest in fighting Goliath? What did this reveal about his own motivations?

4. Why did God allow David to defeat Goliath? What lesson does this teach about God?

᭝ Some Key Principles ᭝

God receives glory from using those who trust Him.

The main point of David's encounter with Goliath is that God can use even the most over-matched person for His glory. David did not win the battle because he had more courage than Goliath; rather, he won the battle because the Lord was on his side. God could have sent His Spirit to empower Saul, as he did in 1 Samuel 10, but then the glory for the victory would have gone to Saul. By using David, the Lord alone received the honor for the victory.

David knew this. While Saul was timid about becoming king, David rushed into battle trusting the Lord. While Saul continually thought that unless he acted a certain way he would lose his battles, David knew that the battle was not his to lose. If David was on God's side, God would get the glory for the victory. Saul spent his life angry because God was not on his side. David spent his life with courage, knowing that he was on the side of the Lord. For this reason, the Lord gets the praise because He is the one who achieved the victory.

Courage is found by trusting in God's sovereignty.

David acted despite any feelings of fear that he may have had, but he did *not* simply charge blindly across the valley, hoping things would work out. Blind action in the face of fear is merely folly, not courage. David was courageous because he knew two things: he would be king over Israel, and the Lord would not be mocked.

Fear grows when we focus our eyes on the things of this world. The Israelite army was terrified because they were busy looking at Goliath and his terrible weapons. David, however, scorned those material weapons. "You come to me with a sword, with a spear, and with a javelin," David said to Goliath. "But I come to you in the name of the LORD of hosts, the God of the armies of Israel" (1 Samuel 17:45). David understood that worldly weapons are powerless against God.

The Scriptures are filled with men and women who found great courage in the Lord. In some sense, those in the Bible who demonstrated the most bravery all are considered brave because of their unwavering trust in the Lord. David knew that he would be king, and so he had confidence in the face of death. David knew that the Lord would not be mocked, so he had confidence in the face of the battle. Courage comes from an unwavering trust that God is in control of our lives. We may fight, but the battle belongs to the Lord.

Obedience breeds courage—in ourselves and in others.

David was a lowly shepherd boy, probably not old enough yet to join Saul's army. This situation might have bothered him somewhat, making him feel left out as his older brothers went off to fight the Philistines. But David had work of his own to do, tending his father's sheep and carrying food and supplies to his brothers in battle. He did not become bitter or resentful in his role as errand boy; instead, he attended faithfully to the mundane tasks his father asked him to do.

It was this very faithfulness that led David, quite unexpectedly, into a situation requiring great courage—and it was this very faithfulness that bolstered his courage to face that challenge. He was already prepared to fight Goliath because he had already been faithful to his father's work, defending his father's sheep against wild animals. David had developed the habit of obeying immediately and completely, and that habit brought him the courage to answer Goliath's challenge. When the Israelites saw that God had honored David's obedience, they responded by shaking off their fear and going into battle themselves. David's obedience bred courage in those around him.

Courage and obedience always go hand in hand. The more we obey the Word of God, the more we will discover that God is always reliable—and that gives us courage to trust Him more. Once we obey Him, our obedience encourages obedience in others around us, and even our smallest acts of courage breed courage in others as well.

⌢ Digging Deeper ⌢

5. *Why did the army of Israel tremble with fear? How could they have gained courage?*

6. What was the source of David's courage? What was the source of Saul's cowardice? What was the fundamental difference between the two men?

7. What would the Israelites have thought if Saul had defeated Goliath? How does the Lord's use of David give Him more glory than if He had used Saul?

8. When have you acted on emotion rather than on faith? When have you acted on faith in spite of strong emotions? What were the results in each case?

⤴ Taking It Personally ⤵

9.   How do you ensure that the Lord gets the glory for the accomplishments in your life?

10. What steps of obedience is the Lord calling you to take this week? How might those steps increase your own courage? Increase courage in others?

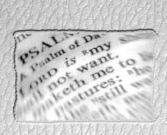

SECTION 4:

SUMMARY

Notes and Prayer Requests

~ 12 ~
REVIEWING KEY PRINCIPLES

⌁ LOOKING BACK ⌁

We have covered an important period in the history of Israel in the previous eleven studies, as the nation moved from the leadership of judges to a long succession of kings. We have seen some great contrasts in the characters: Samuel had a close walk with God, while Eli didn't really know Him at all, causing him to fail utterly as high priest. David possessed great courage, whereas Saul was riddled with consistent fear and ultimately was rejected by God as king. But one theme has remained constant throughout these studies: *God is faithful*, and those who obey Him will grow in faithfulness as well.

The fruits of godly faithfulness are many. One such fruit is loyalty, as seen in the profound friendship between Jonathan and David, which lasted more than a lifetime. Another is respect, which David showed for Saul's position as God's anointed. These things come from obedience to God's Word, not from within oneself. Saul strove to find power in his own will, while Samuel and David found their strength in the character of God.

Here are a few of the major principles we have found in this study guide. There are many more that we don't have room to reiterate, so take some time to review the earlier studies—or better still, to meditate on the passages of Scripture that we have covered. Ask the Holy Spirit to give you wisdom and insight into His Word. He will not refuse.

⌁ SOME KEY PRINCIPLES ⌁

The Lord is pleased by a willing heart.

Samuel was scarcely more than a boy, certainly no older than fourteen, when he heard a voice in the deep watches of the night calling his name. He leaped out of bed without complaining and rushed to his master—only to find that Eli had not called him. When he heard the voice a second time, he did not lie in bed and ignore it; he ran once again to Eli's side. When the Lord gave him some very bad news for Eli, his heart quaked at the thought of delivering such a message to the man who was like a father to him—yet he did so in obedience to the Lord, and he delivered it in full.

Eli, on the other hand, had served the Lord less willingly. When he was faced with the unpleasant task of disciplining his sons, he did not obey fully but only halfheartedly. Samuel's quick and willing obedience, even in unpleasant tasks, stood as a tacit rebuke to the high priest. We saw the same contrast between Saul and David.

The Lord does not want His people to serve Him grudgingly, but willingly and cheerfully. "Take My yoke upon you and learn from Me," said Jesus, "for I am gentle and lowly in heart, and you will find rest for your souls. For My yoke is easy and My burden is light" (Matthew 11:29–30). And 2 Chronicles 16:9 tells us that "the eyes of the LORD run to and fro throughout the whole earth, to show Himself strong on behalf of those whose heart is loyal to Him."

The Lord gives victory in the battle.

The Philistines were a very powerful nation, and their armies were feared throughout Canaan. The Israelites were armed with slings and bows at best, and many fought with simple farm tools. They were no match for the iron weapons and chariots of the mighty Philistines, and their hearts were filled with fear when the enemy gathered in force on their borders.

But their powerful foe could not stand before the wrath of God, and He sent them into confusion simply by roaring out with a thunderous voice. The Israelites still had to participate in the battle on that occasion, just as the Lord does involve His people in spiritual warfare today, but ultimately the victory belonged to Him alone.

God's people still face many foes today, whether from the open hostility of the world or from spiritual attacks of Satan—but the principle still applies: the Lord will defend and protect His people, and He can never lose. It is important to remember what He has done for you in the past, most notably in the sacrifice of His own Son on the cross at Calvary. As the apostle Paul rhetorically asked, "If God is for us, who can be against us? He who did not spare His own Son, but delivered Him up for us all, how shall He not with Him also freely give us all things?" (Romans 8:31b–32)

We are to follow God, not imitate the world.

The nation of Israel was surrounded by pagan nations, many of whom were very wealthy and powerful. It would have been easy to look at their Philistine neighbors and envy their prosperity and military power, and easier still to become tempted by the carnal practices seen in their pagan temples. The people may even have justified such envy with the attitude that, if the Philistines prospered by serving Baal, it can't be all that bad!

In order to imitate another person, we must be paying close attention to that person. In order to imitate the Canaanites, the Israelites had to focus their eyes on their neighbors—and that meant taking their eyes *off* of their God. What we focus on becomes our role model; if we immerse ourselves in the entertainments and lifestyles of the world, we will end up imitating the world.

Christians are to immerse themselves in the Word of God, in regular corporate worship, and in prayer. When we fill our hearts and minds with the presence and Word of God, our eyes will be steadfastly focused on Christ—and we will find ourselves imitating Him. "Therefore be imitators of God as dear children," wrote the apostle Paul. "And walk in love, as Christ also has loved us and given Himself for us, an offering and a sacrifice to God for a sweet-smelling aroma. But fornication and all uncleanness or covetousness, let it not even be named among you, as is fitting for saints; neither filthiness, nor foolish talking, nor coarse jesting, which are not fitting, but rather giving of thanks" (Ephesians 5:1–4).

God demands obedience, not expedience.

Saul obeyed the Lord's commands insofar as it suited his purposes. He attacked the Philistines in an effort to throw off their yoke of bondage, and that was in obedience to the Lord's will. But when the battle became difficult, he did not hesitate to violate the Lord's commands by usurping the authority of God's chosen priests. He attacked the Amalekites and put the people to the sword—but he kept the chosen wealth and plunder for himself.

Both of these decisions might be seen in the world's eyes as simple expedience. Saul was in an emergency with the Philistines surrounding him, and Samuel was nowhere to be found. It was simply expedient that he offer the sacrifices himself. Defeating the Amalekites was sufficient obedience; slaughtering good sheep would have been wasteful. But in both cases, Saul only obeyed in part—and he felt the freedom to choose for himself *which* part to obey.

The Lord expects His people to obey fully, not in part. Difficult circumstances do not excuse us from obedience to the Lord's commands. The Christian's job is to obey God's Word and leave the consequences in His hands. The Lord had not abandoned Saul when the Philistines surrounded him; had Saul waited for Samuel, the Lord would have worked a miraculous deliverance for Israel. He has not changed since Saul's time—He will deliver His people from destruction, yet He expects His people to obey His Word.

Man looks at the outward appearance, but the Lord looks at the heart.

When Saul was anointed king, the qualities the people noticed were that he was tall and strong, standing head and shoulders above his peers. When Samuel met the sons of Jesse, he was immediately taken by the eldest son because he, too, was tall, strong, and very handsome.

Humans tend to believe the evidence of their senses, which is unavoidable to some extent because we live in a physical, material world that is experienced through those five senses. But God transcends the things of this physical world, and He does not see our lives through five physical senses. God looks upon the hearts of people, not upon their outward appearances. He sees beyond our actions and accomplishments, weighing our hearts and looking for people who are determined to obey His Word.

It is interesting that the New Testament gives us no physical description of what Jesus looked like—how tall He was or what color His eyes were. The prophet Isaiah even tells us that "He has no form or comeliness; and when we see Him, there is no beauty that we should desire Him" (Isaiah 53:2). The Lord is not interested in such matters; He is concerned with whether we reflect the *heart* of Christ, devoting ourselves to obedience and faithfulness, and that should be the focus of all God's people.

Mankind cannot thwart the purposes of God.

Saul's kingship was characterized by ignoring the direct commands of the Lord, obeying the parts that coincided with his own plans, while ignoring anything that did not seem expedient. He had the attitude that he was free to reinterpret the Lord's word to suit his own pleasure, and he did not recognize God's sovereignty as being greater than his own.

Yet Saul himself unwittingly furthered the very plan of God that he was trying to ignore. He eventually spent all his efforts trying to cling to the throne that the Lord had taken away from him, but those efforts were utterly futile. He could not prevent the Lord's will from being carried out, and he ultimately even furthered those very plans against his own will.

Saul's attitude is very prevalent, even today. People often pick and choose what parts of God's Word apply to them—if any—and our culture even teaches us that we are sovereign over our own fates. We are encouraged to think that the warnings of Scripture will not apply in our own lives, and that we can do as we see fit without any fear of bad consequences. But the apostle Paul wrote, "Do not be deceived, God is not mocked; for whatever a man sows, that he will also reap. For he who sows to his flesh will of the flesh reap corruption, but he who sows to the Spirit will of the Spirit reap everlasting life" (Galatians 6:7–8).

The Lord is pleased with those who are faithful.

Jonathan and David were men of loyalty and faithfulness. Jonathan was loyal to his father, both as father and as king, and he was also loyal to David as friend and as the future king. Both he and David were completely faithful to their word, and David kept his vow of friendship long after Jonathan had died.

Such faithfulness can often come with a cost. Jonathan was caught in a very difficult situation where his loyalty to father and friend were in conflict. David's faithfulness to the Lord's anointed prevented him from doing any harm to Saul, even though Saul was actively trying to kill him. For Jonathan, the cost of his faithfulness was the throne; as long as David was alive, Jonathan would never be king. The Scriptures are full of men and women who made faithfulness to God their highest priority, even at the cost of their own lives.

Hebrews 11 is filled with many heroes of the faith, men and women who placed their faith in God's word and demonstrated faithfulness to Him throughout their lives. Many "were tortured, not accepting deliverance, that they might obtain a better resurrection. Still others had trial of mockings and scourgings, yes, and of chains and imprisonment. They were stoned, they were sawn in two, were tempted, were slain with the sword. They wandered about in sheepskins and goatskins, being destitute, afflicted, tormented." And what does the Bible say of them? They are those "of whom the world was not worthy" (Hebrews 11:35–38). The Lord is pleased with those who remain faithful to Him.

God does not promise long life or material prosperity.

Jonathan was a man after God's own heart, just as David was—yet both men suffered injustice and hardship. Jonathan died young in battle, dutifully standing by his father the king. David had been anointed by Samuel to take the throne of Israel, yet he was forced to run for his life for many years. He hid in caves, lived with Israel's enemies, even feigned madness once in order to save his own life—yet he was faithful to the word of God.

The Lord does not promise His people that they will be exempt from suffering or hardship or sorrows—in fact, quite the opposite is true: those who follow Christ must expect to share in His sorrows, just as we share in His glory. David and other saints of Scripture understood this principle, so they did not lose heart when suffering came their way. Paul, for example, spent many years in various Roman prisons, even though his deep desire was to be traveling the world as a missionary. Yet his imprisonment led to a large portion of our New Testament.

God's people must not lose heart when suffering comes, for the Lord uses all things in our lives—both good and bad—to perfect His character in us. "My brethren, count it all joy when you fall into various trials, knowing that the testing of your faith produces patience. But let patience have its perfect work, that you may be perfect and complete, lacking nothing" (James 1:2–4).

Those who govern us are placed in authority by God.

Saul was not an effective king. As time went along, his grip on sanity became increasingly tenuous. What's worse, he was plagued by an evil spirit, subject to demonic attack and oppression. He was vastly unjust and was obsessed with trying to murder David—even though David had served him faithfully and selflessly.

Nevertheless, he was the king whom God had anointed over Israel, and all Israel was called to obey him and submit to his authority. The world would argue that David, at the very least, was exempt from this injunction. After all, he, too, was anointed king, and Saul was trying very hard to murder him. Wouldn't it have been acceptable for David to defy Saul's authority, as one peer to another? David's answer to that question was a resounding "no."

The world is not lacking in corrupt leaders and inept politicians, and some Christians around the world are faced with genuine, life-threatening persecution for their faith. But God's Word teaches us that believers are to submit themselves to the authorities whom the Lord has placed us under—even when those authorities are unjust. "Let every soul be subject to the governing authorities. For there is no authority except from God, and the authorities that exist are appointed by God. Therefore whoever resists the authority resists the ordinance of God, and those who resist will bring judgment on themselves" (Romans 13:1–2). The only exception to this rule is when an authority commands one to violate the law of God.

⌁ DIGGING DEEPER ⌁

1. *What are some of the more important things you have learned from 1 Samuel?*

2. Which of the concepts or principles have you found most encouraging? Which have been most challenging?

3. What aspects of "walking with God" are you already doing in your life? Which areas need strengthening?

4. Which of the characters we've studied have you felt the most drawn to? How might you emulate that person in your own life?

ᕼ Taking It Personally ᕼ

5. Have you taken a definite stand for Jesus Christ? Have you accepted His gift of salvation? If not, what is preventing you?

6. What areas of your personal life have been most convicted during this study? What exact things will you do to address these convictions? Be specific.

7. What have you learned about the character of God during this study? How has this insight affected your worship or prayer life?

8. List below the specific things that you want to see God do in your life in the coming month. List also the things you intend to change in your own life in that time. Return to this list in one month and hold yourself accountable to fulfill these things.

If you would like to continue in your study of the Old Testament, read the next title in this series, The Restoration of a Sinner, or the previous title, Finally in the Land.